Ray Evans rescues the issue of ... puts it firmly on the agenda of ... practical, with lots of helpful insights for churches of all sizes. All readers interested in seeing gospel growth in their communities should read this book.
Stephen Gaukroger, Director of Clarion Trust International

Ready, Steady, Grow! is the fruit of Ray Evans's wide reading of both often-forgotten scriptural texts and often-ignored secular literature, and comes distilled through over thirty years of pastoral experience. There are no quick-fix solutions or lazy shortcuts here, but a resource guaranteed to provide church leadership teams with much-needed vision, clarity and on-the-ground help as they seek to labour *and grow* in God's harvest field.
Dave Gobbett, Lead Minister, Highfields Church, Cardiff and Word Alive trustee

Whether we're responsible for small, medium, large – and especially what he calls 'awkward-sized' – churches, Ray has written just the book for us. He has distilled his breadth of experience and depth of reading into brief chapters that are ideal for reading and discussing as a leadership team at any stage or size. Biblical, optimistic and level-headed – this is timely wisdom.
Chris Green, Vicar of St James, Muswell Hill, London, and author of The Message of the Church *in* The Bible Speaks Today *series*

As churches grow, so also problems multiply. *Ready, Steady, Grow!* is an invaluable guide for church leaders, explaining how to navigate the various stages in church life. Ray Evans has read widely and thought creatively about the issue of church growth. More importantly, he has lived out absolute commitment to gospel ministry and service to his own church family over many years. This book is grounded in confidence in the truth of Scripture, and full of everyday examples and common-sense wisdom.
Dr Sharon James, author and conference speaker

As Ray talks about the problems that growing churches face, I felt like he had been secretly spying on our leaders' meetings! He gets it exactly right. As the long-time minister of a growing church, Ray has spotted accurately the problems that assail churches which grow to an awkward size and what makes them stall. With biblical wisdom and pithy insights from his own experience, and plenty of practical advice that is driven and rooted in the grace of Jesus, Ray suggests

an actual system that you can use to plan for and navigate growth. My guess is that any leader of a church that is growing or wants to grow will think Ray has written this book for their exact problems.
Maurice McCracken, leader of Christ Church Liverpool

This is a seriously helpful book for any pastor who wants to see their church grow. It's biblical, wise, down to earth and grounded, full of principled pragmatism. It's thoughtful and thought-provoking, a book full of sanctified common sense that makes you wonder why you didn't see it before. The author's style is to be encouraging rather than critical, so he leaves you thinking, 'If God can do it with Ray in Bedford, he might just do it with me here.'
Phil Moon, Vicar of Bishop Hannington Church, Hove

One of the greatest obstacles to the advance of the gospel in the UK is that so many churches are content to be relatively small. The barriers to growth are often: fear of becoming bigger, lack of vision and lack of effective leadership. If we are to reach the nation, we need churches to grow so that they can reach their communities with the good news about the Lord Jesus. Dr Ray Evans has written this challenging and encouraging book, combining excellent biblical teaching, pastoral insight and godly wisdom. He shares the lessons he has learned from many years of church leadership experience, and through his extensive engagement with cutting-edge Christian and secular literature on leadership. Every church leader, and many church members, ought to read this book. It will stimulate their thinking, raise their expectations and inspire them to consider how they might do more to fulfil God's purpose for local churches.
John Stevens, National Director of the Fellowship of Independent Evangelical Churches

It is estimated that 97% of Britain is unreached by the gospel. Ray Evans sees the local church in dependence upon the Spirit as the critical factor in changing this statistic. In *Ready, Steady, Grow!* Ray provides helpful advice and useful tools to help churches enter and navigate the waters of gospel impact and growth. This book will be a particularly valuable tool for leaders who find themselves perplexed, not only by the challenges of growth, but also by their churches!
Steve Timmis, Acts 29 Global Director

READY STEADY GROW

READY
STEADY
GROW

EQUIPPING TODAY'S GOSPEL CHURCHES

RAY EVANS

INTER-VARSITY PRESS
Norton Street, Nottingham NG7 3HR England
Email: ivp@ivpbooks.com
Website: www.ivpbooks.com

First published 2014

British Library Cataloguing in Publication Data
A catalogue record for this book is available from the British Library.

ISBN: 978-1-78359-113-8

Set in Dante 12/15pt
Typeset in Great Britain by CRB Associates, Potterhanworth, Lincolnshire
Printed in Great Britain by Ashford Colour Press Ltd, Gosport, Hampshire

*Inter-Varsity Press publishes Christian books that are true to the Bible and that
communicate the gospel, develop discipleship and strengthen the church for its mission
in the world.*

*Inter-Varsity Press is closely linked with the Universities and Colleges Christian
Fellowship, a student movement connecting Christian Unions in universities and colleges
throughout Great Britain, and a member movement of the International Fellowship of
Evangelical Students. Website: www.uccf.org.uk*

CONTENTS

INTRODUCTION: A DANGEROUS BOOK?

The Dangerous Book for Boys. Here was a book that grabbed my attention. In fact, I nearly called this one *The Dangerous Book for Church Leaders.* Why? Because it is!

I want to help you grapple with the exciting challenge of growing a church, and leading it (or being a significant player in leading it) through the nerve-jangling difficulties encountered on the journey. Amid the spiritual adrenalin rush, this can easily become a person-centred, systems-oriented, technique-ridden, quick-fix approach that ends up miles away from genuine spiritual progress. It's a heady brew, and the danger is to concentrate on what we can *do*, as if church growth were more about *us*, than the gospel and the Holy Spirit.[1]

Nevertheless, I want to show what can happen in ordinary towns, when normal gospel churches, using everyday leaders whom the Lord Jesus has provided, and in dependence on the Holy Spirit, do what God commands.

Bedford is one such town: nothing flash, nothing remarkable, no large university to provide an influx of young enthusiasm; in fact, no rapid anything happening here. Our manufacturing base has disappeared, replaced by huge warehouses moving on Chinese goods. Our high street is declining, as yours probably is too. Yet our population is growing, soon to be beyond 120,000. Its make-up is wonderfully mixed: according to the town hall blurb, we are 'the most ethnically diverse town in the world'. It's here, in a town like many, that God is growing churches. One of them is ours. You could learn from many others, for nationally we have a significant Christian heritage to draw from, but this is the church and town I happen to know very well.

The challenges I describe are not the common territory of those who write about apologetics and cultural movements, nor are they depictions of the besetting sins of our generation and how the gospel can bring transformation and hope. I am not even going to exhort my readers to more fervent spiritual disciplines, important as they may be. No, I am writing about the spiritual and practical blockages due to confusion, numbers, complexity and complaints.

However, if it sounds as if I am saying 'good method' is the solution, that would be a mistake. I am not lapsing into a false confidence with an emphasis on technique and control alluded to above. Reared on the solid doctrinal ministry of men like Dr Martyn Lloyd-Jones and the thoughtful teaching of Dr Francis Schaeffer, it goes right against my grain to concentrate on what appears methodological or simplistic. Answers with a formulaic ring don't appeal to me at all.[2] But what I am doing is employing biblical insights and common-sense wisdom to help leaders overcome the kinds of difficulties they often tell me they face, but for which they don't get much help.

When the going gets . . .

Christian optimism of the late twentieth century struggled to
come to terms with the tough, unbelieving landscape of the
secular Western world. The resurgence of the Reformed
faith, numerous student conversions in the colleges and universities and the coming of the Charismatic Movement upon
the British scene promised much in the second half of the
twentieth century. Yet they and other spiritual movements
struggled to make much progress against a strong headwind
of wilful ignorance and deep scepticism.[3]

Of course, there are gospel churches in many of the cities,
towns and villages of Britain. The trouble is that most are
really quite small, given the size of their community. We
need, by God's grace, to see 'stalled' churches growing
once again.

I firmly believe that too many churches stagnate in their
growth, or even derail in their gospel proclamation, because
of problems that could be overcome if they just knew how. I
have met many leaders and spoken in numerous churches
desperately in need of help. They do not lack a desire to grow,
but are unsure as to how to take things forward.

What follows has been presented at many seminars, leadership training days and church weekends. It always seems to
resonate. I trust it will resonate with you too, and offer
pointers for action and change.

Right to be wary?

Ian Stackhouse, Pastoral Leader of Guildford Baptist Church,
wisely comments, 'When church life – indeed evangelism . . .
is detached from . . . issues of spiritual nurture, programmatic

and manipulative techniques become commonplace, distorting the shape . . . of Christian self-understanding and Christian ministry.'[4] Many are wary, fearing a theological sell-out to unfettered pragmatism or worse. People have rightly warned about 'the numbers game' and the subtle temptations associated with growing a church.

Others think it is time to move on from an emphasis on growth. It is part of what was trendy a while ago, a throwback to a 'modernist past' and an infantile obsession out of which the church should mature.

In a debate, pitching 'spiritual growth in the blue corner' versus 'numerical growth in the red corner' is commonplace. We fall into the trap of quality *or* quantity, rather than the positive both/and vision of the New Testament.[5]

Furthermore, any mention of 'leadership' raises anxiety. It carries a definite health warning, for it feels it is about over-sized egos and human achievements. Though many leaders are well prepared for doctrinal controversies, pastoral care, personal spirituality and preaching techniques, they have received relatively little help with leadership matters. Many feel out of their comfort zone and area of expertise, vulnerable to the charge of becoming 'mere managers', not 'proper pastors'.[6]

Moreover, whereas the mindset of believers in other countries may be an overt 'can-do', in British evangelicalism it is often 'pietism'. 'Let's just pray about it' is the standard response to a difficulty. That is all that is required for a solution. It might not be put quite like that, but that is in effect the default mode.

Yet listen to God's words to a *praying leader*: 'The LORD said to Joshua, "Stand up! What are you doing down on your face? Israel has sinned . . . " ' (Joshua 7:10–11). Joshua is challenged *to action*.

Necessary and wise advice from a visitor helped Moses overcome a significant practical challenge, even though he was the humblest man on earth. Personal piety on its own couldn't deal with this; organizational wisdom and leaders leading well were required (see Exodus 18; Numbers 12:3). If it was necessary then, it is necessary now.

The journey ahead

With all that in mind, let me map out where we are going.

First, we'll learn how to take a good look at your church and leadership, analysing what might be blocking your way and holding you back (chapters 1–2).

Then we will confront some of those challenges, utilizing biblical and practical wisdom to help you overcome them (chapters 3–4).

Thirdly, we'll use a 'mental map' to focus on what can be done in different areas of church life to foster discipleship and growth, with special attention on winning people to Christ (chapters 5–10).

The conclusion will encourage and challenge you, so that your church is ready, is steady and can grow.

The big picture

In his book about the self-esteem movement, *The Big Ego Trip*, Glynn Harrison rightly reminds us:

> . . . we are all part of something bigger than ourselves. It's not about you or me . . . We are all here to serve the glory of the bridegroom, Jesus Christ. John wants his disciples to see that it

isn't about them. They may well be *at* the centre of God's purposes, but they themselves are *not the centre* of his purpose. God's purpose is to bring glory to his Son, and that is their purpose too.[7]

Within that big picture, I want to tell you about corporate experiences of God's grace and the transforming power of the gospel of Christ. And I want to give you some of the help you need.

What will energize and encourage you to persevere, whatever the challenges you face? The American preacher, John Ortberg, points the way:

Vision is fundamental to the health of your church, but it's probably not the kind of vision you're thinking about.

Someone gets gripped by a vision that will not let them go. But it is not a vision of what they're going to do. It is not a vision of a preferred future. It is not a vision of human activity. It is a vision of what already is. It is a vision of God, and how good he is, and how wonderful it is to be alive and a friend of such a Being.

Out of such a vision flow desires to do good things for such a God. Sometimes these activities may lead to results . . . And then other people may gather, and some decide they'd like to be involved . . . [But] people begin to pay more attention to what they are doing than to the reality of God.

At this point the mission replaces the vision as the dominant feature in people's consciousness . . . people are living under the tyranny of Producing Impressive Results.

The number-one 'vision problem' with churches today is not (as is widely held) leaders who 'lack a vision'. The real problem is when our primary focus shifts *from who God is* (a vision alone that can lead to 'the peace of Christ reigning in our hearts') *to what we are doing*.[8]

As I've said, the last thing I want to do is to fuel a desire, or provide techniques, in order to Produce Impressive Results. But I do want to help you live out a desire to do good things for the God who has loved us and given himself for us. Keep a vision of who he is and what he has done, and this book's advice will be worthwhile.

1. RECOGNIZE THAT SIZE MATTERS: THE GOOD AND BAD OF SMALL, MEDIUM, AWKWARD AND LARGE CHURCHES

One of the most common reasons for pastoral leadership mistakes is blindness to the significance of church size. Size has an enormous impact on how a church functions. There is a 'size culture' that profoundly affects how decisions are made, how relationships flow, how effectiveness is evaluated, what its ministers, staff, and lay leaders do. We tend to think of the chief differences between churches mainly in denominational or theological terms, but that underestimates the impact of size on how church operates.

(Timothy Keller[1])

I thought I knew about small churches (up to fifty people or so). Our church had been there. (It had started with just twelve people in 1972.) Indeed, many other Christians know this reality too, given the size breakdown that statistics reveal. For example, the Fellowship of Independent Evangelical Churches (FIEC), a grouping of over 500 churches in the UK, estimates that its constituency is 69% composed of small churches (memberships of fifty or fewer). In terms of congregational attendance, the overall average is sixty-nine in the morning and thirty-nine in the evening, with a median membership of fifty members per church.[2]

Even in the United States, home of the internationally famous mega-churches, the median church comprises 'just' seventy-five people in attendance.[3] Dave Murrow comments, 'Ninety percent of churches are under 150 on Sunday morning',[4] and Lyle Schaller states that 75,000 Protestant churches in the US average forty or fewer at worship.[5]

This is not a criticism in any way, just stating the fact that many Christian believers live their corporate church life alongside a relatively small number of other believers, and with them seek to take forward what have been called the two challenges given by the Lord to his church, namely 'the Great Commission' and 'the Great Commandment' (Matthew 28:18–20; 22:37–39).

Small is beautiful

Many Christians in churches of this size would say there are numerous plus factors in being small. Indeed, some even adamantly advocate a 'small-is-beautiful' strategy for church life and growth. Small missional communities, it is argued, can reach out more effectively than large, impersonal, programme-oriented churches. For some, small seems more authentic, more New Testament in feel, more manageable, more direct in terms of relationships within the community of faith and more effective in impacting outsiders.[6] Much of this resonates with a postmodern culture wary of the institutional and the impersonal. So, far from 'small = failure', small can be advantageous. Shawn McMullen notes, 'In an age when human interaction is being supplanted by modern technology, many younger families are looking for a church that offers community, closeness and intergenerational relationships.'[7] Ed Stetzer's research has established that 'about 6 million people [in the USA] meet weekly with a small group and never or rarely go to church'; that is, they relate literally to a house church and nothing more.[8]

So what are the positives of small churches?

First and foremost is the strength of the *relational glue* that holds the small church together. 'It's a nice day; why don't we have a church picnic?' can be an on-the-spot decision at a Sunday morning meeting. What's more, most people will come as part of wanting to maintain group cohesion. When our church was this size, we would have a games afternoon in the local park. Everyone came, to play or watch, those in their eighties and those still in prams! The sense of togetherness was palpable.

Typically, members will socialize with one another as well as meet formally. And even formal meetings can have an informal air about them, with members being glad that they don't have to watch time as their larger-church cousins do.

Everyone knows everyone else. At its best, this means that each and all get prayed and cared for during life's joys and sorrows (Romans 12:15). New people are easily recognized, and the scale of this seems manageable. The church can spend time praying for those they know and love who are not yet Christians. And when somebody becomes a believer, the group can meaningfully rejoice as a whole.

A second strength is shared knowledge. Often there is a shared belief-and-values system to which members subscribe deeply. New people are helped to adopt these, either by a formal process ('This is our doctrinal statement which we all believe'), or informally through tacit knowledge (people picking up what is expected through an assortment of verbal and visual cues). The power of group behaviour means that people either align themselves or soon pull away.

Thirdly, it is obvious that a small church has to work together to maintain itself: tasks are shared out and often done together. It may be arranging chairs in a member's home, contributing to a lunch, looking after someone's child during a talk or clearing up after coffee. If the small group has grown beyond a home's capacity (in the UK, given the relatively small size of homes, this can happen quite quickly), there will be many tasks to accomplish for the Sunday worship service to function.[9] Even a relatively small church may soon have to hire, buy or build. This, in turn, can be another opportunity for developing binding relationships.

Another advantage is a communal sense of sacrifice. Financial expenditure becomes a shared bond, when the small church pays for things *together*: a building to meet in, expenses for visiting speakers, help for a needy person in debt or a child in another continent requiring health care. The finances are not just lost in a big impersonal system, and this kind of pooling of resources will strengthen the group.

I could talk of other benefits too, and so could you if you are in a small church.

It all sounds idyllic, and some Christians from small churches will tell you that it is. Yet you know what is coming: the proverbial 'but'!

Small may not always be beautiful

Why so? The big issue for the small church is that it doesn't and can't easily stay that way. Even if numbers remain about the same, people will inexorably age, young children will grow up and pressure will increase on all those 'shared' things. The group will have to face problems associated with its size dynamics, perhaps sooner than it would like to think.[10]

So what are the negatives of small churches?

Cohesive small churches?
Even some of the positives can, after a while, become negatives. For example, small-group cohesion can become a problem. The military historian, Richard Holmes, described how small-group unity can work against the mission of the overall organization if members lose heart and work together to reinforce poor behaviour traits. And group members will generally fight for one another, but not if the group mindset becomes negative. Holmes refers to Marc Bloch's observation of soldiers in small groups when he says:

> I believe that few soldiers, except the most noble or the most intelligent, think of their country while conducting themselves bravely; they are much more often guided by a sense of personal honour, which is very strong when it is refined by the group. If a unit consisted of *a majority of slackers*, the point of honour would be *to get out* of any situation with the least harm possible.

Holmes adds: 'In short, the creation of group spirit is no guarantee of military performance, for there is every chance that the group's norms will conflict with the aims of the organization of which it forms a part.'[11]

Similarly, small churches might find themselves feeling quite comfortable in their small and cosy world. Their purpose tacitly becomes keeping the group 'as we like it', rather than seeing themselves as a means of fulfilling the Great Commission and pushing hard to make more disciples.

If a leading light or a group-within-the-group sets norms of belief and behaviour other than biblical ones, then the small group can become what some have labelled toxic.[12] The small church becomes hardened to its missional calling, unwelcoming to outsiders who might challenge things and unwilling to adapt to a changing world. Small groups are notoriously prone to the excesses of immature or doctrinally unbalanced leaderships, and may end up feeling like the minor fiefdom of a dominant personality.

Rewarding small churches?

Another problem is that repetitive tasks can feel onerous and unrewarding. Results may appear meagre, and the group may feel like giving up because of a lack of sensed effectiveness. Others just ignore this and soldier on, but with little honest assessment of their own cherished practices. I recall visiting an established church which had seen better days. There were about twenty in the congregation (spread around a building that seated 600 or more). The weird thing was the insistence on a children's talk, for which I had to come down from a very high pulpit and along a back corridor, and re-enter the auditorium to speak to . . . one child! Members at the core of a small church, unchanged for a number of decades, have become both worn down by the continuing demands of keeping it going and used to seeing little growth.

Effective small churches?

Another problem has to do with the numbers dynamic of small groups. In one sense, a group of over thirty is not really a small group at all, but has already progressed to a size where cohesion and loyalty work differently. Fascinatingly, studies in small-group cohesion all put the 'small number' somewhere between five and twenty. After that size is reached, taking part, doing things together and keeping unity just change the dynamics. Holmes' studies suggest that army fighting units have coalesced around this small-group number for many thousands of years. It seems to be the size which can achieve tasks with everyone being part of it.

'The importance of *the primary group of ten*, whose members were in regular face-to-face contact, was recognized long before psychologists or sociologists had turned their attention to the question of group behaviour,' says Richard Holmes. He goes on to describe the Macedonian battle order where soldiers manoeuvred in groups of eight or four. 'In every case, though, the pikeman fought between comrades he knew well.' The Roman army was organized around ten eight-man mess units (the *conturbenia*). Over 1,700 years later, the Prussian army was formed around the seven-man *Kameradschaft*, and the British army today still fights as units of small squads.[13]

So a church that feels it is going to maintain effectiveness as it grows from twenty to around fifty has already lost some of the greatest benefits of small-group intimacy. Medium to large churches, through a well-run small-group structure, may actually be reaping more of the benefits of this form of organization, and may be able to motivate and disciple people more effectively than small-church advocates may realize. Ed Stetzer argues that because today's large churches emphasize small groups and community, thus creating a small-church feel, they offer the best of both worlds.[14]

Vulnerable small churches?
Another issue is the group's vulnerability to small fluctuations in numbers. Core members often will nervously think, 'It will only take one family moving away for us to lose viability.' One

couple with children move in, and it feels wonderful. Yet if that happens in reverse, disaster. Without realizing it, small churches invest a huge amount of energy in retaining people. The unspoken contract is: 'Please don't leave, because if you do, you may be responsible for closing this church.' Leadership's goal becomes keeping people, whatever the cost. If change might upset a group member, the group won't change.

This pattern of behaviour doesn't happen overnight, but develops with the passage of time. Sometimes desperate leaders are tempted to adopt a very controlling and directive approach to pastoral care.

Church trends commentator, Peter Brierley, notes in his analysis of the 2005 English church census, 'The smaller the church, the much more likely it was to have declined; virtually three-quarters, 74%, of the smallest churches did so . . . 53% of them declined very fast.'[15]

Small becoming something else

If, however, the small church does see growth, it faces a stark choice. Does it plant again, now that the group has grown to around forty, by 'splitting' into two groups of twenty, for example, or does it grow into something larger, say a medium-sized church of fifty or more? That's no bad thing to face up to, but it does need some clear thinking.

The greatest challenges come from two things: the provision of leadership and the instability of the dynamics of groups of a certain size.

The provision of leadership

Where does one small group find enough good leaders to take two groups forward? Many churches of forty would struggle to support one full-time leader financially, never mind two. Most groups of twenty certainly wouldn't be able to do that. Now it is easy to say at this point, 'Leaders need to be open to the reality of being "tent-makers".'[16] That is absolutely true and valid. But if we adopt the plan that small churches will grow to just about medium-sized, where they then plant small again (and then again), the leaders will likely face a lifetime of being tent-makers. That may well be a necessity in some places, yet it is a big ask – especially so if the church aspires to have well-trained leaders committed to the theological, missional and leadership training required to take it forward.

It seems a waste of capability to have gifted men leading very small churches, with no real expectation that they will ever be supported by their members financially and devoting lots of time to doing something else to earn a wage.

I was a window-cleaner for two years, with over 400 houses on my books. It was an honourable and necessary job, and I studied when it was raining. Then I was released to only have to clean windows for three days a week, as the church could afford to pay for two days. By some marvellous providence, I was contacted by a distant acquaintance to do research for the Regional Directorate of the EU. Overnight, my status changed: I officially became a consultant! This too was an honourable post (even if you are a Euro-sceptic). But I found it all very tiring. I was trying to squeeze too much into my limited hours. My mind was always on both jobs at the same time. It was a privilege eventually to be fully supported so that I could concentrate on what God had called me to and gifted me for. Tent-making may well be a sacrifice some have to make, but I think we need to be wary of playing down how hard it is.

For some, the solution to the finance problem is to find outside money, gaining support from larger churches elsewhere. This is hard to sustain over a long period, however, and churches that stay small do not support full-time workers. The early Brethren system turned this reality of small-group life (non-stipendiary elders) into an almost mandatory biblical requirement, seeing it as a blessing, not a curse. Others have realized that it may not result in well-trained leadership, and the small church can end up being led by well-intentioned, but not necessarily capable, preacher-leaders. Alternatively, the small-church leader who does want to be supported may be in danger either of exerting undue pressure on members to give to the cause (namely, his salary) or of being nervous about mentioning money at all, because it is so personal.

The instability of small-sized groups

One answer to the problem of small-group instability is a model that keeps such missional communities working together as they grow and replicate, and meeting together as one ('the gathering').[17] This plan is really more a method of growing a large church, consisting of large sub-units: the size dynamics, financial requirements and leadership provision will mirror those of a larger church. It is important to be aware of this, so that leaders can grasp the likely size problems they will face, rather than ignoring them.

Growing large small-group sub-units will bring its own tensions. When we, as a church at one phase of life, sought to keep three large sub-groups of twenty to fifty organization-ally together, we found it very difficult to maintain cohesion once new people started coming and shaping things. New-comers didn't relate to those parts of the church that met in different places from their own. Each group soon began to develop different characteristics. Though we tried, we could not keep the groups under one umbrella for long without difficulties surfacing. As groups reached a critical mass of more than thirty people, there was a strong desire to order their own values, make their own decisions and appoint their own leaders. In a sense, they began acting as *churches* do, rather than as small groups do.

In the end, one group became a separate sister church, and the other two groups recombined and started meeting together as one medium-sized church.

If we had maintained a strong, controlling type of joint leadership, things might have been different. But the key issue affecting this developmental stage is the point where group aspirations and decision-making responsibilities coalesce. This is especially so once it has its own distinct leadership, recognized or appointed by the *group*, rather than imposed by others. Though an organization can maintain cohesion for a while, once such leaders really start leading on their own initiative, then a new church is birthed and it may want to go off (sometimes rapidly) in a different direction from its mother church.

To maintain other patterns will require exerting a more authoritarian style over the groups than may be justified from the New Testament. In the later decades of the previous century, when this plan was experimented within the so-called 'House-church' Movement, this became one of its major problems.

Medium-sized church bliss

An expanding small church which does not quickly opt to plant another small church will find itself growing into a medium-sized church with around fifty to a hundred and fifty attending. A church plant which starts with, say, thirty people could realistically look to doubling its attendance as the

horizon for which to aim. To see that in seven years would
mean growing by 10% each year. To be part of it all is exciting
and encouraging.

Yet even if small churches don't see quite that kind of rapid
growth, many do experience a positive sense of going forward.
If there is spiritual warmth, a faithful commitment to the
gospel and to the Bible, and there are people seeking to serve
God and others, many will have a sense that 'the good hand
of the Lord is on us' and will grow spiritually and numerically.
The church may aspire to be part of what's been called the
'tipping point' of a 10% Christian presence in a community.
A church in a small village of a couple of thousand would
want to aim for an attendance of a medium-sized church or
beyond.[18]

A whole host of positive factors emerge which often lead to
more growth. The church has now got past its vulnerable
stage. So, for example, the church can afford a full-time worker,
if it hasn't got one already, or pay the one whom some other
church has supported. It will have a more regular meeting
place or even its own premises. It will likely have developed a
stable leadership with recognized office-bearers.

As well as these institutional markers, there are other great
benefits in crossing over into a medium-sized church. There
are now more people around to do the work, and the church
can branch out into new things, leading in turn to more
people being attracted. Children and young people attend,
and even if not in great numbers, at least they are now present.
When a couple with children visit, they will see others like
themselves and won't feel the odd ones out.

Jobs can be shared around, and people can specialize, using
their gifts. Whereas once it was 'everyone takes a turn', now
there may be some capable musicians to help with the
worship. The church can afford better publicity and become

more recognized in the community. New people are more willing to be involved. The church leader may get invited to speak at local schools and he now has the time to do so.

There are also positive *human* dynamics. People still know everyone else's names. New people can be recognized, talked to and cared for. One church leader claims that if a church works at three quality indicators: namely quality welcome, quality teaching and quality hospitality, it will normally grow. A medium-sized church can provide all three. Whereas a small church might feel a bit intimidating or odd for a newcomer, and the teaching might just be a bit ordinary (for example, a sermon starting with the disclaimer: 'Sorry, I have been really busy and had to prepare this in a hurry late last night'), a medium-sized church is sufficiently large to feel like a small crowd, intimate enough to be personable and well enough organized to be attractive. A large church might struggle at the hospitality and perhaps the welcome aspects, even if the teaching is great.

For a church leader, the medium-sized church can be bliss. A good pastor knows each and every family's history, visits everyone comfortably in a reasonable time-span and is personable with established members and newcomers alike. Such a people-friendly character can be a huge attractor to the church. People feel that they have access to him. His (and his family's) kindness is very strong relational glue for newcomers. Indeed, leadership capability in small and medium-sized churches will often boil down to good people skills, taking the church quite a way forward.

Decision-making can often be consensual, and the church may experience a great degree of unity if it is led wisely. The pastor can consult informally, and people will feel they are being listened to. All can take part and thus gain a sense of ownership. Decisions are 'we decided', not just 'they decided'.

Many pastors and church members feel very content with this size of church, especially if it has grown this way. Indeed, some would like to freeze it there as it is. It's a bit like having a ten-year-old daughter – she enjoys being that age, hormones haven't kicked in, boyfriends haven't arrived, she isn't out until the early hours, and so you as parents enjoy life too!

But nothing stays the same

But can churches stay like this indefinitely? A church that has grown to medium-sized will experience a real sense that the numbers work for it, yet certain things can make this more difficult. One is that the church keeps on growing! It becomes the victim of its own success, and difficult size dynamics arise. (More anon.) The other is that it doesn't end up staying that way *really*. Two downsides emerge, as follows.

Church weaknesses

It can be difficult to be in a medium-sized church if it keeps like that for several decades. Why? The main reason is that the gospel-driven desires of Christians get blunted by what they experience. Whereas once the church saw growth, now converts are few and far between. People do not think that people they know will ever become believers. Why? Because they are making judgments based on decades' worth of watching the church have relatively little impact.

Churches begin to turn inwards on themselves. 'The pastor's job is to tend the flock,' becomes the members' concern. Of course it is, but the tyranny of the 'either/or' can set in, rather than embracing the 'both/and' of shepherding *and* evangelizing (see 2 Timothy 4:2, 5).[19]

It is so attractive to be medium-sized, compared to what comes next, that many leaders and churches begin, almost without knowing it, to shy away from moving on. Long-term medium-sized churches are like some middle-aged couples. They become stuck in their comfortable ways, adopt a conservative attitude to change and can lose their sense of what brought them together in the first place.

Leadership struggles

Leading such a group can be difficult. Even without church hassle, the pastor sees the changing age demographics working against the health of the church. Couples get beyond child-bearing, and once-young families are soon bereft of their children, leaving many an empty nest. Formerly strong core church members begin to feel personally what the ageing process of Ecclesiastes 12 is all about.

But it can be even more challenging than just that. An aspiring preacher once expressed to me a strong desire to go into full-time ministry. 'You do know it is all about conflict resolution in one form or another,' I told him. 'The preaching is the nice part of the job.' Sadly, many a pastor of a medium-sized church with a problematic history will know all about this. Often a power structure has developed, meaning that the key opinion leader calling the shots is not the full-time worker, but the head of a clan or network who has been there for some time.

Lyle Schaller, in his (somewhat dated, but still very useful) study on church dynamics, identified from a sociological perspective that tribes typically have a tribal chief, a chief medicine man and an administrator to help them function. In some ways, churches function like small tribes. In many a medium-sized church, the minister will be the one bringing the bulk of the teaching of beliefs, values and ideas (aka the chief medicine man). Yet there may be a head of a family, to whom others look for guidance, one who embodies what the church really holds to (aka the tribal chief). When these two 'posts' are not held by the same person, conflict often results, and the chief medicine man rarely wins![20]

Medium-sized churches may experience a rapid turnover of senior leaders or even end up in a cycle of 'hiring and firing'. Once the average term for a minister in the UK was only seven years. In Francis Schaeffer's early years in the USA, it was about two![21] That tenure period has increased, but if a church is pastored for a short period only, it can be very difficult to lead it through significant change and growth.

Many settle for maintenance mode. Yet it just could be that with extra help and training, leaders might encourage churches into another phase of gospel growth, and reinvigorate members with expectancy and hope.

The A-sized church, with a grade 'D' for difficulty

I thought there was just one more category – small, medium and of course . . . large? No, I discovered that there is the awkward-sized church! What exactly is that? It's the size in which, no matter how hard a full-time pastor works, things seem to come unstuck. Even the highest capacity worker will struggle with much more than 150 attending, unless things change. Indeed, it takes more than leaders with good people skills to take the church through this phase.

Could this glass ceiling be why many churches remain the size they are? Could this be why many plateau and then slowly decline, with lots of frustrated members, as they approach this size?

The awkward-sized church needs exploring in some depth. Whereas there is a lot written about planting and growing small churches, there is little help for leaders at this point. Now is when important leadership skills need to emerge and some very big 're-engineering' changes have to happen if the church is to go forward – either into a larger-sized category or into vigorous church planting.

The awkward-sized church (about 150 to 400 attendees) will present three main problems, and it will not feel as if it provides many positives to its members for some time.

Problem 1: mindset

Essentially, the problem is this: the church is growing beyond everyone knowing everyone by name. For many, belonging to a church in which this happens is a sure sign of relational failure, and for some even a mark that the church is straying from a biblical pattern. In a medium-sized church that is slowly growing, this creeps up on people. To start with, core people keep expanding their network circles to connect to new people. The pastor may work hard, spending extra time with visitors. He may exhort members to be better at welcoming, better at talking to people they don't know and better at hospitality. But the church which had been so good at embracing the new, the needy and the neglected begins to fear that such people are now falling through the cracks.

Compounding this, new people don't even start to get to know everyone; they realize that this is a receding target. They settle into the habit of talking to people like themselves, those with whom they most naturally connect. Many, attracted by the positive aspects of a healthy church, just benefit from what it offers. To core people, these new members seem to be part of a growing fringe that doesn't commit to helping in the way that everyone had to do when the church was growing from small to medium.

People are coming up against the thing they assume is true of a large church and which they fear is happening to them, namely that the church, *their* church, is becoming impersonal, and consumed by a chasing after numbers.

Many conservative evangelical Christians in the UK seem to have a strong aversion to such growth pains, and the thought of their church *really* growing is not what they desire in their deepest heart, whatever they may say.

Problem 2: leadership capability

The pastor now feels that the visitation and counselling and organizing of the growing number of meetings are becoming past him. Everyone still wants him to be their personal pastor/ chaplain. He will have to work at speed; what is going to get missed? Which of the many spinning plates is going to crash to the ground first? What else will fail? Will it be his health or his family life? Will there be a sharp comment to a disgruntled person? By now there are quite a few of those, as people are raising all kinds of concerns, in short: 'The church isn't what it used to be!' It all seems so bizarre: 'We have prayed for growth for so long, so how come it feels so *negative?*' This is the unspoken question that many, including the pastor, are asking.

The leadership of a church approaching the awkward size will begin to notice the organizational complexity. Larry Osborne, an American pastor who has written extensively about this issue, talks about leadership teams that were once very small-scale. He describes the sole pastor being like a 'track athlete', with members cheering him on to perform well. That moves on to a form of leadership which he likens to 'golf buddies', where a small leadership team is built around

RECOGNIZE THAT SIZE MATTERS   35

personal friendship, shared and tacit understandings of many
key spiritual issues, and where decisions are made informally.
This gives way, in the awkward-sized church, to a leadership
structure more akin to a basketball team, where there are
some specialists and roles which are clearly mapped out, and
where orders are given and taken by the other leadership
'players'. Finally, he likens a large-church leadership structure
to an American football team with its offence, defence and
special teams (a UK equivalent might be a rugby union team
with its front row, backs and fullback). If a 'track-athlete' sole
pastor is to change his leadership style to manoeuvre through
all these required leadership level changes, this will take
some adjustment.[22]

Problem 3: organizing tasks

On top of this, one of the great frictions in the awkward-
sized church is the way work gets done. Typically, in smaller
churches, active members often have their fingers in many
pies and will be aware of most things going on; this dynamic
structure works really well. It is impossible to make this work
now, because what brings stability to a smaller church will
stifle the progress of an awkward-sized one. So, as it transitions, the church has to make one of its biggest structural
changes: no-one can possibly know all that is going on, no-one
can meet all the needs, yet jobs still need to get done.

Without knowing how to handle this issue, the leaders will
be blaming all the wrong people or the wrong things. We
will see how to negotiate these serious structural problems in
several of the next chapters.

The strong temptation is to ignore all of this and just enjoy
the benefits of no longer being small and struggling. David
Anderson has observed that medium- and awkward-sized
congregations tend to lose the evangelistic focus they once

had, and instead adopt what he calls a 'club mentality'. 'You
have just enough people not to be missional anymore [and]
you don't have to grow anymore to sustain your budget.'[23]

Having 'just enough' – did you spot that? It's the subtle
danger. Enough people to get the jobs done and pay the bills,
enough work to keep one pastor busy, enough visitors to
create the impression that mission is happening, enough
problems not to want any more. It takes a strong sense of
urgent purposefulness not to want to stay in this relatively
safe place, but to tackle the challenges of growing the church.

However, if the temptation to become self-satisfied can be
resisted, the church may, by God's grace, grow large.

Can big be beautiful too?

In the UK, it seems that 'large' begins somewhere around 400
attendees. The category can stretch to about 2,000, after
which it becomes a mega-church.[24]

This is the size at which everyone realizes they aren't going
to get to know everyone's names or even necessarily recognize
their faces. Yet this no longer causes consternation. Most
people rejoice at being in a meeting that has such a crowd and
don't see it as a negative, so long as the church also works
at creating relational places such as small groups. (More on
this anon.)

The church may still have the same doctrinal confession, a
similar values code and style of worship, but it will all feel very
different indeed from when it was small. There are pluses and
minuses of being large, but I suspect that lots of Christians
from small or medium-sized churches can't imagine many
pluses at all. Only small is beautiful, and large is ugly, foreign
and not very missional. But let me list a few positives.

Positives

Firstly, the 'footprint' that a large church leaves in a community is huge. It has massive and complex networks, and vast numbers come into contact with the faith through these. At a large church, you may spot the man who cleans your windows, the girl who serves you at the check-out, the nice lady doctor whose surgery you attend, the teacher your children smile at when they say, 'Hello Miss', and the guy in the office next to yours. For secular people, used to the marginalization of Christianity, this comes as an eye-opening revelation: 'I never realized that so many people I know are "into Christianity".' This helps people feel that it is not all odd.

Secondly, a large church has the power and capacity to organize significant community-impacting events, as well as mercy ministries. If a large church has a heart for its community, then everyone from the local mayor to the man who found help when he came out of prison will know it is there. The church should be so much a part of the flourishing of the community that non-Christians begin to say, 'We can't imagine our community without you.'[25]

Thirdly, there is an attractive power in a large church organizing things well. There will be a large number of entry points for those with differing interests, abilities and concerns, helping individuals to faith in Christ. The church can plan to help unbelievers access what they need in an environment that will assist them the most. Services will often help create a plausibility structure (what some sociologists of religion have seen as a big challenge in commending faith to secular people).[26]

Whereas a small church tends to work in practice on the maxim that like attracts like, the large church can make the most of attracting an array of people, knowing they will find both 'people like me' and 'people unlike me'. Both these factors attract: one says, 'You are not alone'; the other visually and powerfully says, 'Christianity's point of unity is the gospel, and not some other phenomenon such as race, class, educational attainment, age or work status.' This reinforces the claim that the gospel is good news *for all*. Whereas a small church proclaims this, a large church also *demonstrates* it.

Fourthly, the large church can produce excellent aesthetics, from its front-door website to its back-door office administration, from its well-trained speakers to its engaging welcome team, from its tasteful decor to its excellent coffee, from its terrific musicianship to its heartfelt prayers.

Of course, we should remember, as the great Christian thinker C. S. Lewis powerfully reminded us, that the Lord accepts our worship not because of the quality of what we offer, but for the intention. It is an offering of love, much like a little child will use her daddy's own money to buy him a present he doesn't need, but which he will treasure for the rest of his life. It's the love that counts.[27]

We ought also to remember that when any church of any size meets, it joins in with that vast number around the throne already worshipping the Lord (Hebrews 12:22). The largest mega-church pales into insignificance compared to that gathering, and the smallest church can lift its head high.

Nevertheless, because worship is both vertical and horizontal (a time when together we worship 'our Father in heaven' but also edify one another here on earth), the quality of the aesthetics counts, and sometimes for visitors it counts hugely.

While churches of any size can plant, large churches have the necessary resources and expertise to facilitate this. Often they have a wide geographical spread of members and can set apart some from a particular area to start a congregation. Larger leadership teams can spare gifted preachers to pioneer the plants, and the church will have finances to support these through their early years.

A large church can also deploy its other resources wisely and for gospel-driven reasons. Teaching a larger group, for example, can be a better use of resources than the alternatives. A capable, gifted Bible teacher may as well speak to a thousand as to a hundred or ten. There is no dishonour in speaking to any size of group, but the wise use of scarce resources (money, time and ability) means that growing a large church may be better than developing many smaller churches, all of which need gifted speakers and leaders to take them forward. One church of 1,000 will invariably have capable Bible teachers bringing God's word to many people. But it will also have many other workers leading gospel initiatives, for which smaller churches would not have expertise or resources. If church life were organized around a different principle (say ten churches of about a hundred), each church would spend virtually all its money on a Bible teacher and renting or buying a place to meet. Bible teachers might find themselves constantly duplicating in a small area. And the gospel might well not advance as successfully in the latter case, with resources being ploughed into maintenance rather than growth.

Large doesn't have to be impersonal. In a small church, you will know the other thirty people by name, work with most of them, be friends with perhaps a dozen and be close friends with three or four. In a medium-sized church, you will know all seventy-five by name, work with about thirty of them and have about a dozen friends, three or four of them close. In an awkward-sized church, you will recognize the faces of perhaps 200 or more, know the names of 100, work with thirty and have no time for friends! In a large church, you won't recognize them all, but you will still know 150 or so by name and work with a team or two so that you rub shoulders with thirty people. You will know about a dozen well through a home group and you will have time for close friends. A large church can offer the relational benefits of the small, but added to that is the tremendous encouragement of seeing a large crowd gathered under the Word of God and many coming to faith in Christ. So large may not be as lonely as many fear.

Relationships can develop in large churches. Boys can meet girls, single people be affirmed in their calling, workers encouraged on their 'frontlines', and people whose lives have been messed up in all kinds of ways can find support.

Other pluses abound. It doesn't take much imagination to see the vision of winning many to Christ becoming an exciting reality.

Large size, big problems

But are there downsides? Of course! Number one is that a large church is just a large group of forgiven sinners, not a large group of perfect people. Indeed, it is so often full of people with personal problems that resources are stretched to breaking-point.

The large church is subject to all the problems that large numbers bring: organizational accountability, adequate resourcing, quality assurance, coherent decision-making, effective communication, responding quickly to crises, adapting appropriately to change, to name just some. And getting lost in the system is always a threat.

In the small church, the *relationship* is what connects. If the music is poorly done, it doesn't matter too much, because everyone knows that Aunty Joan is lovely and without her sacrificial help we wouldn't have music at all. A visitor can be told this and appreciate the point. In a large church, visitors in particular will know nothing of this. They will just hear poor music and wonder why. This goes for every area of the church's ministry that visitors will see. They can't connect easily to the relational, only to the aesthetic. This is true for the preacher too. In a small group, the fact that he is such a nice person will mean people will listen to his sermons; in a large group where many don't know the preacher well, he has to connect through good ministry.

It isn't easy to improve the aesthetics of the church's main meetings as it transitions from medium through awkward to large. In a small church, aesthetics seem unimportant, and some people will wonder why they should matter as the church grows. They may even see the move to improve quality as the church becoming more commercial or worldly. Some may struggle to improve that much in any case. We all have capacity and capability, but sometimes a task gets beyond our ability, no matter how much coaching we are given. And to ask one person to step down from a ministry so that someone better can take their place is a huge cause of difficulty in transitioning churches. Indeed, it takes enormous grace on everyone's part. For when a change has to happen, it uncovers whether someone has been serving the Lord for his glory alone or whether their identity and significance has become wrapped up with the work they do. Taking away that role may seem to question their very worth. If they have subtly made service the source of their personal meaning and value, then difficulties arise when it has to be laid down. A large church will have had to face up to these issues and overcome at least some of them. The church needs to teach about this so that the matter is handled well.

Large can sometimes breed 'superior'. Jim Collins, in *How the Mighty Fall*, a secular book on what causes large organizations to fail, speaks also to the church. It is frightening to hear that the slide starts with 'hubris born of success', moves onto 'an undisciplined pursuit of more', then 'a denial of risk and peril', followed by a 'grasp for salvation' and finally a 'capitulation to irrelevance or death'. In his excellent book, *Building below the Water Line*, senior leader Gordon MacDonald relevantly unpacks these aspects for every church. It makes for sobering reading.[28]

The takeaway

So what have you learned from our foray into the four sizes of churches? Much, I hope, that resonates with you, whatever size of church you are involved in. You may have recognized some of the dynamics. Had you ever come across their significance before? I hadn't, until someone pointed out that the stresses our church was undergoing could be related to size pressures.

But it's not enough to describe the pressures, is it? I needed to know what God wanted me, and our church, to do about them. So do you. That's what the rest of this book is about.

Do you recall what God said? There are 'more than a hundred and twenty thousand people who cannot tell their right hand from their left . . . *Should I not be concerned* about that great city?' (Jonah 4:11, emphasis added). If God is concerned, we must be too. No discussion of church size can be academic; the growth of your church is about Jesus' honour and about people's desperate need being met by the magnificent news of the gospel.

Discussion questions

1. What size is your church? Count the number of people who come on a reasonably regular basis (say once a month or more). That figure will tell you the kind of size-dynamics issues you are facing better than just a membership number or the size of congregation at any one meeting. And what are the trends – steady, up or down (and how fast for either) over the last year, five years, ten years? What have the trends meant for your church? Are there any other special trends in the demographics: more young adults, new parents or older people than in the past?

2. Armed with that knowledge, discuss the pressures changing numbers have put on you. How are these manifesting themselves? Are there complaints? Is there a frantic pace to everything or confusion over what's happening, or is there a feeling of decline with 'nothing' apparently happening?

3. Look at the different-sized churches around you. What can you see that they might be unaware of? What might they see in your church that you can't easily recognize or won't confront?

4. Why are churches other than those of our own size a bit threatening to us, whatever size we are? I have met people from small churches who would hate to be large, and vice versa. Why's that? What problems can this present for leaders?

2. SEEK WISDOM: THRIVING AS THE CHURCH GROWS AND LIFE GETS COMPLICATED

How can your church overcome what is holding it back and go forward more confidently?

You could do no better than listen to words spoken to a great leader, facing serious pressures that had the potential to derail everything: 'What you are doing is *not good.*'

Moses is the man, and Exodus 18 is the story. This surprising element in the plot-line develops when a man named Jethro visits Moses at a time of crisis. To feel the power of what God is saying, note the setting. It's a part of the Bible where God regulates so much: detailed laws about all kinds of things, given to the people of God so that they would be a 'kingdom of priests' to show God's great glory, wisdom and grace to the watching world. Immediately after this visit comes the giving of the law at Sinai, with all the seriousness with which it was recorded (see Exodus 19).

Detail was important. Francis Schaeffer made the point that even the specified colour of the pomegranates on the high priest's robes had a purpose.[1] The people of God were to take these seriously. Nadab and Abihu, sons of Aaron, the first high priest, ignored what the Lord said: 'They offered unauthorised fire before the LORD, contrary to his command' (Leviticus 10:1–2). Their presumption that they could worship God in any way they wanted, and not as he commanded, led to an act of severe discipline and them being punished for this act of treason. It taught all the people of God that what he says as our King is paramount, and there are times when, for the good of the whole community, his judgment comes upon the disobedient.

It's into this context of God the King giving serious, detailed instructions to his people to order the whole of their lives that the narrative introduces Jethro as one bringing vital wisdom. This enables them to cope with organizational complexity. It's as if God mandates listening to wisdom, even if it comes from a surprising source.

Jethro's solution to Moses' problem

Who exactly is Jethro? We are introduced to a non-covenantal person (a priest of Midian) and Moses' father-in-law, someone to whom Moses has sent away his wife Zipporah and his two sons. Jethro thinks the place for the wife and children is with their husband and father, and he brings them back to Moses and talks to him in no uncertain terms (Exodus 18:6).

Moses rehearses all the Lord's goodness to his people, at which Jethro rejoices. Non-Israelite though he is, he responds by offering burnt offerings and confessing with his mouth the Lord's supremacy.

The next day, Jethro sees what Moses can't: the organizational mess affecting the administration of justice. Moses is working hard, seeking to implement God's will for his people. But Jethro knows that Moses' working pattern isn't the answer. Moses and all the people are 'wearing themselves out' (see Exodus 18:18). Moreover, this 'isn't good'; it is 'too heavy' for them, and 'they 'can't handle it alone'. This all tells us they are mired in a serious problem.

The solution? Listen to good advice! This is human insight garnered from Jethro's more detached observation and his years of experience. Advice alone is not enough, though; it needs the ongoing blessing of God. Jethro adds, 'May God be with you' (Exodus 18:19).

Note that he doesn't say, 'Go and enquire of the Lord for more laws to get an answer for this.' Nor does he say, 'You will just have to work harder.' (How many leaders have tried that one over the years?) Rather, what he proposes is an organizational solution; teach them God's ways and plan for a system of care which is manageable. People with lesser problems can see someone at that small-group face-to-face familiarity level. So, appoint 'leaders of tens' (see verse 21). Notice that number again: there is something about a small group being significant, as human organizations have proven for millennia. But then after that, there is a small-church level of a leader of fifty, a medium-level of a leader of a hundred and then a leader of a thousand.

Wise leadership is good leadership

The text emphasizes that the quality of leadership is critical (verse 21): 'capable men . . . who fear God, trustworthy men who hate dishonest gain'. They can then 'serve' (verse 22). Character clearly counts as well as gifts. The New Testament endorses this same emphasis on godly leaders (see 1 Timothy 3; 2 Timothy 2:2; Titus 1).

Elsewhere we see Solomon seeking the key ingredient that will make him a great leader of God's people. He asks for wisdom. In his prayer, he acknowledges that, without this, who would be able 'to govern this great people of yours' (1 Kings 3:9; 2 Chronicles 1:10)?

So wisdom is not merely a skill thing, nor is it just about being smart. It is always godly, moral, humble and servant-hearted. James tells us, 'But the wisdom that comes from heaven is first of all pure; then peace-loving, considerate, submissive, full of mercy and good fruit, impartial and sincere' (James 3:17).

Jethro is teaching an already-good leader some new things that he really needs to learn. Moses is willing to eat humble pie and listen (verse 24) and then make sure it's implemented by doing 'everything he said'. It doesn't take much imagination to think of other things you might say about a father-in-law as you pack him off home when he has made you look a little foolish about your vocational competency. But Moses listens to wisdom, and so should we.

Jethro just disappears off to his own country (verse 27: note again the hint to remember that he isn't one of the covenantal people on his way to the Promised Land) and also off the pages of history too. It's his one and only appearance, but how significant it proved to be. Moses got his life back; the people of God were governed and led well, and today we are being instructed about being wise!

In this passage, God mandates listening to wisdom from an outside source. If you slightly changed the names and circumstances, this could easily be an account of an external consultant brought in to do a quality-assurance check on a struggling organization coming up with recommended changes, a kind of Ofsted 3,500 years ago.

This truly was a missional piece of good advice, for 'the nations' would take note of all of it. As Moses came to the time of his departure, and the law was given for the second time, he said:

> Observe them carefully, for this will show your wisdom and understanding to the nations, who will hear about all these decrees and say, 'Surely this great nation is a wise and understanding people.' What other nation is so great as to have their gods near them the way the LORD our God is near us whenever we pray to him? And what other nation is so great as to have such righteous decrees and laws as this body of laws I am setting before you today? (Deuteronomy 4:6–8)

The stakes were very high then; they still are today.

Three sides to leadership

We can characterize the ministry of a leader as consisting of 'prophetic' teaching, 'priestly' compassion and 'kingly' governing.[2] The leader himself must ensure he is growing in all three aspects.

I want to concentrate on the last part of that, for a lot of help is available elsewhere for theological and pastoral training. These are necessary and important, for leaders must 'correctly handle the word of truth' (see 2 Timothy 2:15), and this is no easy task, because the Bible is a large and complex book, and people's difficulties are legion. Wisdom, faithfulness and skill are needed to teach it properly, and to help people compassionately.

In the Jethro and Moses story, the wisdom/leadership aspect is emphasized. This is an area where many contemporary church leaders feel their lack. The church doesn't do much teaching or investing in the whole area of leadership.

One seminary I know is just starting a leadership track after many years of neglecting it. Another has a leadership track for students, but until recently it wasn't mandatory, and only 40% of the year-group opted for it.

But note that when the Salvation Army did a major research programme examining what factors were influential in taking the church forward, they found it wasn't those often mentioned, like great buildings with big car parks, a vibrant youth work, close proximity to a university or a good location in suburbia. No, strong leadership and clear vision were the key factors. Researcher Peter Brierley comments, 'A church without an effective leader will discourage rather than encourage attendance.'[3]

This comes to the fore time and time again in churches of all sizes. Put godly, capable leaders into almost any situation and, given God's good grace, they will take the work forward. That's why almost any scheme can be made to work. It's not so much the particular plan which is the silver bullet, but the quality of the people leading it.

In the New Testament there are those with gifts of leadership who must 'govern diligently' (Romans 12:8). Supremely, our King Jesus has 'the government . . . on his shoulders' and 'of the increase of his government and peace there will be no end' (Isaiah 9:6–7). Significantly Paul didn't just write to the Philippians; he sacrificially sent Timothy to help them so that they might see what selflessness looks like. Paul sent someone of whom he said:

> I have no-one else like him, who takes a genuine interest in your welfare. For everyone looks out for his own interests, not those of Jesus Christ. But you know that Timothy has proved himself, because as a son with his father he has served with me in the work of the gospel.
> (Philippians 2:20–22)

Paul *modelled* the characteristics of another Father who gave and sent, and Timothy *modelled* what it meant to be a son coming selflessly in the service of the gospel, just as another Son did. So the people not only heard but saw what disciple-ship should be like.

Power, leadership and common grace

There are obviously dangers associated with leadership and power. Leadership is about pleasing God and not caving in to be like everyone else. Remember the Israelites' call for a king, so 'then we shall be like all the other nations, with a king to lead us and to go out before us and fight our battles' (1 Samuel 8:20). They got what they wanted, a man 'a head taller than any of the others', but alas, he did not have a heart after God's own heart (see 1 Samuel 10:23; 16:7).

Jesus had a very different view of line-management than the rulers of this world. He emphasized that church leaders must not mimic those who use power for their own ends:

> . . . a dispute arose among them as to which of them was
> considered to be greatest. Jesus said to them, 'The kings of the
> Gentiles lord it over them; and those who exercise authority over
> them call themselves Benefactors. But you are not to be like that
> . . . I am among you as one who serves.'
> (Luke 22:25–27)

Servants we are and servants we should be, even as we lead.

Suspicion may also arise because of a misunderstanding about biblical teaching. A strong doctrine of what theologians call 'common grace' and a clearer understanding of what they dub 'the regulative principle' (the teaching that we should only worship God as he himself has instructed) will help us see that God encourages us to mine for wisdom. There will be the equivalents of Jethro today; the question is whether or not we are willing to let them come and help us, and whether we will listen to what they say about what they see, which we can't see.

Two important doctrines: common grace and the regulative principle

Common grace is the teaching that God is good to all that he has made, including those people who don't acknowledge him. The goodness of God to them means that they are not only kept from being as evil as they might be, but are actively given gifts and qualities of character to enrich life. Some have great insights into overcoming problems, including problems with running an organization.[4]

The regulative principle is an outworking of the second commandment. It also connects to the doctrine of 'the sufficiency of Scripture'. This teaches that God's Word contains all we need to know for 'life and doctrine' (1 Timothy 4:16). It 'thoroughly equips us for every good work' (see 2 Timothy 3:17). The church isn't left rudderless or having to rely on tradition, experience or reason for its sources of authoritative teaching and behavioural obedience.[5]

This doctrine doesn't negate the gaining of wisdom from external sources, for the sufficient Word teaches that we can gain help by listening to wisdom where it is found. Wisdom is not to be rejected if not specifically found in the Bible, for, as the Word itself shows, we can benefit from the insights of others. The moral status of this kind of wisdom is always at the level of advice. It is not a binding moral imperative, but it is still important.

It's worth learning too from the careful thinking of previous generations of Christians. For example, in James Bannerman's thorough treatment of church power in his book *The Church of Christ*, he says that where the church is dealing with something 'in common with the practice of any civil and well-ordered society among men', the church can decide some issues 'by the aid of the light and law of nature'. He goes on to discuss Paul's injunction: 'Let all things be done decently and in order' (1 Corinthians 14:40 KJV), an important text in helping us grapple with this matter. He then quotes the Westminster Confession of Faith: 'There are some circumstances concerning the worship of God and government of the Church, common to human actions and societies, which are to be ordered by the light of nature and Christian prudence, according to the general rules of the Word . . .' He then refers to similar passages in other great Confessions of Faith.[6]

Two helpful leadership insights

Here are examples of common-grace wisdom, found in the comments made by two leading coaches, both now knighted in recognition of the wisdom they have brought to their respective sports.

Sir Clive Woodward talks about the importance of 'critical non-essentials'. He makes the point that winning the Rugby World Cup in 2003 was not just about the game on the pitch, but about the food preparation, team rules that instilled in players a discipline of working for one another, providing contact with home, and a thousand and one other things that helped the England players perform better on the pitch than any other team.[7]

In a church worship meeting, for example, there are a lot of critical non-essentials. If the building is too cold, the sound system is poor, the seating is uncomfortable, there's no welcome for visitors and refreshments are non-existent, the ability to concentrate and engage will be affected. Are these things essential to salvation or the church accomplishing its goals? No. Are they a source of putting people off? Yes, they can be. So why put extra barriers in the way? The only barrier we want people to stumble over, if they stumble at all, is 'the offence of the cross' (Galatians 5:11). If aesthetic and environmental aspects can help or hinder, why not have a good look at what helps in your situation and do something about those things you can improve.

Sir David Brailsford, the architect of British cycling success in the 2012 Olympics, talks about 'marginal incremental gains'. He points to the importance of working on improving a whole host of small things by a mere 1% margin. So, for example, better sleep results from each cyclist using the same pillow wherever the team happens to be staying overnight. Add all these marginal gains up and the upshot was that UK cycling virtually swept the board of medals.[8]

So where are your 1% improvements going to be? Our church was challenged to do 1% more praying on a Saturday evening, take fifteen minutes more out of the day to commit Sunday to God, and make 1% more smiles – it's amazing what a smiling face does to someone's sense of being welcomed! Finally, we were encouraged to eat 1% more food, as long as it was with someone else during the week somewhere. Meals eaten with others make a difference. Read Tim Chester's excellent *A Meal with Jesus* if you're unsure of the missional value of food.[9]

Can't some of the wisdom of these two coaches be harnessed in your church?

Wisdom about change

Another zone where we need wise insights is in managing change. For change is inevitable if a church is to grow and then keep growing through the size categories. In *Vintage Church*, Mark Driscoll puts it like this:

1. Growth causes change.
2. Change causes complexity.
3. Complexity causes chaos.
4. Chaos causes concern.
5. Concern causes conflict.

Driscoll comments:

> This conflict comes in eight different forms. With each form, a person or a faction of people want something they perceive that they have lost due to change. They fight to preserve what they lost and in so doing oppose change. Their efforts focus on gaining or regaining one of eight forms of church currency that they value . . . Such change can be perceived by some as a loss of power, remuneration, preference, information, visibility, role, sustainable pace, or control.[10]

Change is not problem-free!

Many leaders find this aspect of leadership one of the most difficult, an area where they feel worn down or worn out. Help would be welcomed.

A quick stats lesson for church leaders

The help comes from the humble bell-shaped curve, so beloved of statisticians. The uptake or numbers of adoptions of innovations can be plotted over time, and often the resultant graphs have a familiar bell shape. What is more, researchers have found that if the people who adopt are studied, trends emerge. Some people show characteristics that mean they are open to change, but others, for a variety of reasons, are opposed and will adopt only reluctantly.

The following is a typical outline of how researchers have described adopters.[11] An innovation adoption could be anything from buying a smartphone to visiting a new IKEA store. People don't leave their temperamental and decision-making style behind at home when they attend church members' meetings!

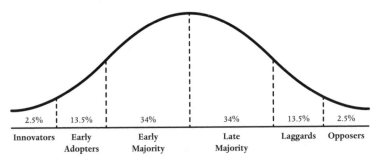

2.5%	13.5%	34%	34%	13.5%	2.5%
Innovators	Early Adopters	Early Majority	Late Majority	Laggards	Opposers

Figure 2.1: Openness to change patterns

So why is this so important? Because some people are temperamentally more negative than others about innovation and change. Typically, as you can see from the diagram, they amount to about 16%. In many churches, there are at least 2.5% who are not just laggards, but temperamentally are *against everything*. If a church puts its voting threshold for a decision at 80%, this negative group will only have to persuade a few other people to vote with them, and the motion will fail. In effect, a negative minority rule the church. In a small church, this might represent a handful of negative people running the church. They don't have to have plans of their own; they can just vote against others' plans for change. So the status quo will be kept, and the church may stagnate.

Often, a leader will be so aware of these people that he will spend an inordinate amount of time trying to overcome their objections and get them on side. That may be work that needs to be done. Remember the explorer Sir Ernest Shackleton's good practice of what amounted to 'Keep your friends close, keep your enemies closer still' when he led his crew after the ill-fated *Endurance* expedition. Simple, kind human contact with the group's difficult people helped him lead all to safety. This too can help us to keep people with us, whatever challenges we face.[12]

But a leader must also spend his limited time engaging with early adopters, those people who view change positively. These are often people who are open but who wisely consider things. If they see the case for change, they will significantly influence the 68% 'majority people'.

These are the people looking both ways – neither hugely positive nor negative about change. They take their cues from others whom they look to for guidance. If an early adopter they respect offers a strong voice and positive uptake, they will as likely as not adopt it themselves. It's no good looking to 'majority people' for a very positive endorsement; they are not like that. When there is a spread of opinion, they like to be somewhere in the middle: not too much for, and not too much against.

Conversely, if the negative minority have a strong voice, the majority people will not want to upset them, and so resistance to change can build very quickly once the majority begins to be influenced by 'laggards'.

In a church members' meeting, with a vote looming at the end, many a leader struggles with all of this in front of his eyes and ears, often to his dismay. Votes that can turn on tiny fluctuations, biased towards the negative because of a high threshold, have often held the church back from making wise decisions, or meant that the church was much more cautious than it needed to be about innovating for gospel-driven growth.

Leading change well

Is there a better way? I think there is. I was left a genius of a constitution that tries to do two things well at one and the same time, with leaders leading positively and members being consulted and gaining ownership of decisions. Typically, the Independent Free Church stream has been dominated by a 'one-member-one-vote' system, which seeks to do justice to the second principle, but I think it does so at real cost to the first. Other forms of government give leaders a lot more power, but sometimes leave members feeling outside the decision-making process.

So what is a wise way forward? Taking as his starting point the 'Council of Jerusalem' recorded in Acts 15, the nineteenth-century Scottish church leader William Cunningham brilliantly described the balancing act that this passage exhibits between elders leading and members being truly consulted in matters that affect the life of the church.[13]

Speaking personally: a helpful constitution
For our church, this led to an emphasis that elders must lead by teaching according to the clear principles of the Word (for Christ rules his church through his Word). They must give sufficient scriptural arguments, fair reasoning and proper examples for a suggested change.

Members are brought into an open consultation process, something that is often done much better one-to-one to give enough time for people to express their concerns and for a leader to answer objections properly.

After that, when it comes to the decision, elders make a formal proposal, and members have the right to dissent *if they can show scriptural grounds for doing so*. Leaders have a right to assume people will support or at least give them the benefit of doubt (see Hebrews 13:17). So we ask, 'Does anyone dissent, and on what biblical grounds?' This means young and as yet untaught Christians don't positively have to decide on a complex issue or express an opinion on a person or subject they know little about. It helps the 'middle majority' not pretend to be more positive than they are, and also helps them not to be negative unless they genuinely are and have a biblical basis for being so. Finally, those who may be described as 'laggards' are helped to ground any objections they may have in a doctrine or passage in the Bible, and not in personal temperamental whims. With an open Bible, all can put their point of view fairly and honestly, and it is the Scripture that decides, not force of personality, or just positive or negative personality types.

The constitution puts it like this:

> The meetings also give the elders and deacons the opportunity to share their ideas and plans. Open discussion and personal communication with leaders on all aspects of church life are welcomed. In following the teaching of the Bible and through discussion of how it applies to us, the church together seeks to discern the 'mind of Christ' for the church.
>
> At members' meetings sometimes formal decisions are made and ratified. Important issues that affect the life of the whole church, for example the choice of elders and deacons, or affect the church's witness to holiness such as the approval of financial accounts, are brought to the whole church. Unanimous consent is sought on these issues.
>
> The authority invested in elders is an authority which is to be consistent with the Bible's teaching, and so consent is obtained by a fair use of biblical arguments. Church members have the right to dissent from the actions of the eldership if they show sufficient scriptural ground for doing so.[14]

If there is no biblical basis for dissent, we all go forward together.

When church constitutions aren't so helpful

What if you have a constitution that doesn't operate like that? Then work with your key opinion leaders, sometimes called 'gatekeepers'. Engage with them properly, and they will help lead the majority. Often if those people are being helped forward, most of the last 16% or so will go forward too, resulting in a significant majority for most things.

Is this to negate all spiritual values or the validity of arguments put fairly and well? Of course not. The above is not a commentary on the rights and wrongs of a case. The Bible decides that. Most of us know, however, that many decisions are about wisdom, preference and taste. People often vote on what they would or would not like, far more often than on what is morally absolute. This wisdom of how to take change forward brings some sanity, and churches can make progress without it all becoming rancorous.

Could we live our Christian faith out without this particular insight? Of course. Has it helped take things forward? Yes, I believe so.

To summarize, this chapter has shown that we can positively look for wisdom from a variety of sources to help deal with the complexities that develop at different sizes. Such wisdom has to be used carefully, but Moses provides a good example of listening and learning, and the people of God were the better for it.

The New Testament too gives us an example of Christian leaders demonstrating great insight into overcoming a problem that could have wrecked gospel ministry. Do you know what it was? More significantly, do you know what they did, and why understanding that is so crucial for you today?

Discussion questions

1. As a team, discuss what each of you learned about leadership (plus and minus) as you grew up from child to adult, and which you bring to the table now.

2. What other insights from the common-grace world of leadership have you come across? How might they be wisely harnessed in the life of the church?

3. How does leadership work in your church? What are the advantages and disadvantages of the ways it happens where you are? What could help your leaders be more effective in achieving the goals that Christ gives to his church?

4. What problems have you encountered trying to change things? In the light of this chapter, is there anything you might have done differently, or at least faced differently, given a better understanding of how people respond to change?

3. ACT COURAGEOUSLY: ENSURING YOUR CHURCH OVERCOMES DEADLY PERIL

Ever had that sinking feeling that just as things were going well, trouble was coming your way? 'What's going to go wrong next?' is the question. All too soon, it becomes: 'Now what am I supposed to do about *that*?' as a maelstrom breaks on your church.

Three hammer blows hit the early church too, not long after it was birthed. Satanically assaulted, dangerously counter-attacked, in peril of seriously veering off course and splitting up, the leaders had to navigate it through 'a perfect storm'.

Acts 4 – 6 has 'WARNING – BEWARE' written all over it. But great leadership lessons are there too, summarized by the apostle Paul: 'Be on your guard; stand firm in the faith; be men of courage; be strong. Do everything in love' (1 Corinthians 16:13–14).

Any leader will need the help this part of the Bible can give. And it needs unpacking in some detail. Without this, you may conclude that Acts 6, for example, is just a passage that teaches that the church ought to appoint deacons!

A vicious counter-attack on three fronts

To start with, we need to be aware of the differing nature of the attacks (see 2 Corinthians 2:11). Acts 4 presents us with 'external persecution' and Acts 5 'internal corruption' (maybe pretty obvious), but Acts 6 gets under our defensive radar with 'diversionary confusion', caused by organizational complexity and its resulting difficulties. They are met with a variety of defensive countermeasures. We need to understand these if we are to take our stand successfully against the 'wickedness in high places' (Ephesians 6:12 KJV; see verses 10–20).

Acts 4 and external persecution

The apostles are speaking in the name of the Lord Jesus and telling everyone the good news of what God has done in Christ. They are warned off doing this by some of the most powerful figures in the land (Acts 4:5–6). This threat is serious and could stop the fledgling church in its tracks. Indeed, the apostles had seen how the very same people had abused their power to engineer the death of Jesus just weeks before. Their threats were not idle; their authority was real; their power could be utterly destructive.

The church around the world today is still attacked by the evil one in this way. Attacks range from petty bureaucracy making life tedious to prejudice against Christians by those in authority, right through to unjust laws, fines, imprisonments, beatings, torture and death. Persecution is a brutal and nasty experience and an effective form of stopping gospel progress. We are told to stand with our brothers and sisters who are suffering this attack of the devil (Hebrews 13:3).

Another round of attack is recorded (Acts 5:17–40), ending with a flogging for Christ's servants. By repeating the themes of opposition from those in places of high authority (see Acts 5:28, 40b) and intimidating threats of physical violence (see Acts 5:33), Luke is saying to the church, 'This happened to them; it could easily happen to you. Be prepared!'

How did the early church react? They 'raised their voices together in prayer to God' (Acts 4:24). They confessed their faith in the Sovereign Lord who controls all things and they prayed for courage. They experienced an amazing fresh filling of the Holy Spirit and were enabled to speak boldly. The section ends not with a bullied, cowering and defeated church, but with the good news spreading everywhere (Acts 5:41–42).

Yet we are never far away from another outbreak of persecution in Acts. Soon, the first martyrs will be recorded and the church will be scattered by it. The book will end with one of Christ's apostles, Paul, under house arrest in Rome (Acts 28:20 – note the 'chain'), but having the opportunity boldly to keep speaking of God's wonderful work in Jesus Christ – the last word (Acts 28:30–31).

Persecution will remain a vicious tactic until the Lord's return, and the church must know how to draw on our spiritual resources to stand against this particular satanic scheme.

Acts 5:1–11 and internal corruption

Here we are presented with a stern lesson in church discipline, emphasized so that the people of God don't end up being just like, or worse than, those who don't believe in Jesus. If Satan can't frighten the church into silence, he will try to nullify it by causing moral scandal. If the church reeks to the surrounding world because of compromises with evil, then 'job done'. People will never listen to the good news because what they see of hypocrisy, and worse, will deaden them to the message. Many long-established churches know that a whiff of something scandalous can effectively wreck a testimony, often for decades.

The three great temptations of the world are 'dodgy sex, dodgy money and dodgy power'. Hebrews 12:14–17 and 13:4–8 bring these dangers to our attention. If you can get a church leader sexually compromised, and so cause notoriety in a community, why bother to try to change the law of the land to ban the faith? The church has sadly been rocked by a never-ending stream of such sad episodes, and gospel progress has been seriously harmed.

Here, though, the attack is 'dodgy money'. A Christian couple, Ananias and Sapphira, are tempted to be dishonest. It is a satanic attack on them and the church (Acts 5:3). Of course, they were not forced to give all the money away from the sale of their land, as Peter makes very clear (Acts 5:4). Perhaps they wanted to impress others by their apparently heightened spirituality. Perhaps they had seen and coveted in their hearts something akin to Joseph's endearing nickname of 'Son of Encouragement', which we are told about in the immediately preceding section – and that's not an accidental placement by Luke (see Acts 4:32–37).

This is an echo of another event when God's people were taking territory for the Lord and someone wanting to get rich quickly compromised the mission utterly and brought shame and disgrace on all (see Joshua 7; 1 Timothy 6:9–10). Achan too 'saw [and] coveted' (Joshua 7:21). He also was severely judged, so that the people of God would not become a 'stench in the nostrils' of others, and so that all would know that God is holy, utterly good and righteous. Those who mirror him to

others must 'be holy as he is holy' (see 1 Peter 1:15–16). This
is a key meaning of the command to glorify him (see 1 Corinthians 10:31 – 11:1). Note there the close connection between
glorifying God and having a missional impact on others.

They would have known this lesson. It should have warned
them of the danger. But it was lost on them. What about us?
Even if we know these things, we must actively watch out that
they don't catch us out. Flee from them! (1 Timothy 6:9–11;
see also 1 Corinthians 10:6ff.)

If the evils of coveting, lying and hypocrisy had gone on to
become acceptable parts of church life, the general populace
would have concluded, 'You are no different from us, and your
gospel doesn't do what you claim. If you are back into a right
relationship with God, it doesn't look like it.' No wonder Paul
was heartbroken when later a young church began to tolerate
such moral compromise (see 1 Corinthians 5).

In these cases, the best way to respond to such a serious
attack on the church's ability to proclaim the gospel is through
church discipline. Here it is severe and a direct work of the
Spirit of God (Acts 5:5, 10). It's the first case and designed to
warn the whole church, which should realize that Christians
may go to heaven early if their lives are bringing such disrepute
on the gospel and ruining its effectiveness (see also 1 Corinthians 3:16; 11:28–32). Most of the time, church discipline is
about exercising 'the power of the keys' and will mean admon-
ishing, and sometimes suspending or even excommunicating,
seriously disobedient Christians from membership. (See
Matthew 16:19; 18:17–18; 1 Corinthians 5:5, 11; 2 Thessalonians
3:6, 13–14.)

Church leaders must realize just how dangerous tolerated
moral compromise is to gospel progress. Dealing with the
situation requires humility but also boldness and courage.
The apostles realize they are up against a dangerous foe

and can't pussyfoot around. That doesn't mean we become arrogant judges of others (see Galatians 6:1), but it does mean we shouldn't duck an issue that could ruin our gospel witness.

Acts 6 and diversionary confusion

So far, so good. The church has come through two serious counter-attacks with flying colours. D-Day has arrived and the beachhead is secured. It's as if the 21st Panzer division has counter-attacked with its tanks near Caen and the *Fallschirmjäger* troops the other side of Bayeux, but both have been beaten off! The Longest Day has been a success, with the decisive battle fought.

The victory of the cross meant that liberation was being proclaimed and experienced by new people every day (Acts 2:47b). Then loomed one of the most serious dangers of all, not least because it came from an unexpected direction. A fierce storm nearly swamped the Allies in 1944, and the church in AD 30, and threatened to force both back into the 'sea'.

Let's look in detail at Acts 6:1–7 using five 'p' headings: pain, priorities, plans, performance and pointers.

Pain

The church was experiencing *growing* pains 'in those days when the number of disciples was increasing' (verse 1). That's why it was all so unexpected; it came as the church was really succeeding. The pain was then expressed: 'the Grecian Jews among them complained against the Hebraic Jews because their widows were being overlooked in the daily distribution of food' (Acts 6:1). That's a loud alarm call!

Perhaps you don't realize what kind of alarm is sounding and just how loud it is. What Luke describes is bad news because it delineates what could easily become a terrifyingly

destructive fault line. It has ethnic, linguistic, cultural, preju-
dicial and emotionally loaded overtones. We all know how
serious the charge of institutional racism is, and this is a
first-century equivalent in the making.

No-one likes a slight on their background. Though I am an
Evans, when, in a game of rugby union, I enthusiastically
support the two countries (England and Ireland) where most
of my immediate ancestors come from against those from
Wales, the 'land of my fathers', I receive fairly black looks. It's
only banter, I know, and it's only a game.

Yet when the issue is serious – 'my old widowed grand-
mother is going hungry because you leaders are [deliberately?]
neglecting her' – then fierce, gut-instinct rivalries surface. The
complaints made the leaders look incompetent or worse. If
this is not dealt with, the one people of God could split right
down the middle. What kind of witness is this to 'one body
and one Spirit . . . one Lord, one faith, one baptism; one God
and Father of all, who is over all and through all and in all'
(Ephesians 4:4–6) when people in Jerusalem might see two,
and at odds with each other?

The apostles were in danger of getting distracted from the
gospel. It's like a nasty street-by-street war has taken over from
the war of quick movement out in the countryside. Are they
going to get 'bogged down in Caen', as the Allies were for
months after D-Day? Ask any church leader and he will tell
you that sorting out a discipline issue such as Acts 5 can be
distracting and tiring enough, but a potential church split, as
in this section, has us reeling. And what suffers most? The
progress of the gospel. All our energy goes into keeping the
church from tearing itself apart, as members go sideways with
their moans (as they so often do instead of obeying Jesus'
direct command in Matthew 18:15). It may well be what sends
leaders to early graves more than anything else.

Leaders dealing with moaning people
And that's not the worst of it. 'Complain' is a significant word.
It has a history. Let me ask you: when was the first time the
newly liberated people of God moaned about food, indeed
bread? What happened then? It looks as if Old Testament
history is repeating itself before our very eyes. The newly freed
people of God were moaning about food then (see Exodus 16:2,
7, 8, 11; Numbers 11:1, 4, 10), and they provoked God 'exceedingly' (Numbers 11:10). All Moses could see was trouble in
every direction (Numbers 11:10–11), so much so that he wanted
to die to get away from it all (Numbers 11:15). Some church
leaders now, going through a painful time as they watch the
work fall apart in front of them, will know exactly how he felt.

Here the new-covenant people of God seem to be doing
the same. (Luke significantly uses the same word here in Acts
6:1 that the Greek translation of the Hebrew Old Testament,
the Septuagint, uses for 'grumbling' in Exodus 16.) What a
disaster, for whereas the deliverance by a Passover lamb from
Egyptian slavery was important, it was only a model of a
far greater deliverance by the true Passover Lamb from a far
worse kind of slavery. Surely those who have received the
Lord's full spiritual salvation (see 2 Corinthians 3:7–18) won't
repeat the same mistake? It looks as if they do. Last time, it
led to forty years of getting nowhere fast, as they wandered
aimlessly in the desert. Ominously we are told 'their bodies
were scattered over the desert' (1 Corinthians 10:5). We are
not beyond doing as they did, and Paul says, 'These things
happened to them as examples and were written down as
warnings for us, on whom the fulfilment of the ages has
come. So, if you think you are standing firm, be careful that
you don't fall!' (1 Corinthians 10:11–12).

That puts verse 1 into perspective, doesn't it? What a deadly
threat growth pains can bring to a church. This might not

appear to be as serious as external persecution or internal corruption, but being distracted by the problems of complexity can as surely lead to gospel derailment as anything else.

More maths lessons for church leaders

Acts 6:1 has another significant lesson. It points to the link between growth and pain. Many Christians pray for growth, say they want people to become Christians and long to see their church experience this. Yet, when it comes, why does the leadership just end up with a larger in-tray of people complaining? This is such a common experience for churches transitioning through the stages of numerical growth. We get what we long for, and when it comes, it's so hard to cope with and can hurt so much.

Partly it's just a numbers thing. For example, in a conversation of three people, there are six possible lines of communication (you to me, me to you, you to them, and so on).

Driscoll has highlighted what begins to happen as the numbers change:[1]

- A church of 50 people = 2,450 links
- A church of 100 people = 9,900 links
- A church of 200 people = 39,800 links
- A church of 300 people = 89,700 links
- A church of 400 people = 159,600 links
- A church of 1,000 people = 999,000 links
- A church of 6,000 people = 35,994,000 links!

Let's think about that. A church of fifty people has 2,450 links or lines of communication. A church of 400 people has 159,600 possible connections – just eight times larger but over *sixty times* more 'complex'. That kind of rapid complexity growth means that things, and especially people, can get neglected. Moaning is the way that the problem surfaces, not people spouting mathematical equations. The complaints were only a symptom; the real problem was the organization being overwhelmed by the demands on its leadership and structural resources.

No wonder leaders and members struggle. Remote is how leaders feel; remote is how members see them. Problems emerge as organizations grapple with the complexity of how everything works in this new world of changed-size dynamics: information, communication, organization, connections, decision-making, identification, deployment, accountability and individuality.

Priorities

Knowing no better, it would have been so easy to respond differently, wouldn't it? 'Don't you know how hard we are working? Don't you know that there are more important things to do? Don't you realize that your moaning is jeopardizing and distracting the church from its mission?' These are just a few typical reactions. I can think of many more. When we hear a moan, too many of us see it as a personal criticism, feel that our busy life and heavy workload is being overlooked and we are being taken for granted. Most leaders of any length of service would say, 'Been there, done that, got the T-shirt!' Our instinct, at the very least, is to justify ourselves.

Some of us stand on our status. These men could easily have reminded everybody, 'Don't you know we're apostles? We saw the risen Lord. We have personally delegated authority from Jesus, therefore we command you to stop moaning!' They didn't. Acts 6-type problems don't need a remind-them-of-your-authority sort of solution (even if we do need to be very conscious of our priorities as preacher-teachers).

Now here's the *huge* thing. These threats need to be diagnosed carefully. Why? If you treat an Acts 6-type problem with an Acts 5-type solution, woe betide you if you are a grumbling widow! It would have been so easy to misdiagnose, especially given the Old Testament background. This looked and sounded like the same thing, but it was not. The apostles did not discipline the moaners. It would have been so tempting to do so, but so catastrophically wrong.

How many times have leaders, when under pressure and hearing all the moaning and feeling the danger for the church, applied the wrong remedy? There is a way to deal with Acts 6 growth pain, but it is not an Acts 5 method. The disciples, instead of rebuking the people, actually realized it was a different problem and came up with a way forward.

A wise way forward
They realized that they had to fight on at least two fronts: 'Word *and* Deed'. It is easy to misread their comments in verse 2: 'It would not be right for us to neglect the ministry of the word of God in order to wait on tables.' This can sound like a no-brainer! How can you even put those two acts in the same sentence for comparison – preaching God's everlasting gospel compared to hearing '*Garçon*, bill please'? Surely no-one who had been saved for eternity by the good news of Christ would ever want to distract any-body into something as menial, trivial and non-essential as 'table-waiting'. Yet that would be to miss the point of what the disciples are saying.

The apostle John put it like this:

This is how we know what love is: Jesus Christ laid down his life for us. And we ought to lay down our lives for our brothers. If anyone has material possessions and sees his brother in need but has no pity on him, how can the love of God be in him? Dear children, let us not love with words or tongue but with actions and in truth. This then is how we know that we belong to the truth, and how we set our hearts at rest in his presence whenever our hearts condemn us.

(1 John 3:16–20)

They were faced not with an either / or, but with a both / and.[2] Helping some of the neediest people in their community (and widows were among the most vulnerable) was not an optional extra, but an expression of their faith and love. Not to feed the hungry among them would have been a denial of all that they proclaimed. But they still had to get the Word out; the gospel had to get to other people too.

The evangelical church has looked at this plenty of times over the last century.[3] The key to grasping their solution was their understanding that the church had both to speak *and* act, but they, within that mission task, had their own personal priorities for which they were gifted and called. It was about establishing some organizational order to accomplish the twofold task, rather than elevating one to a high priority at the expense of the other. It was not Word instead of Deed, or Word at the cost of Deed, or Word with Deed following a poor second (or vice versa for any of these). It was Word and Deed, but with the apostles focusing on their own priority of prayer and Word (verse 4).[4]

At this point, I have heard some evangelical ministers say, 'Problem sorted, leave Deed to others, so that I can retreat into the study and then go and do some Word ministry. Please don't distract me with anything else; this is my calling.' They might believe this passage justifies that. But no. Not so fast. The passage hasn't ended, nor has it been thoroughly examined yet.

Plans

Having established two priorities for the church as a whole, and their own personal ministry priority, the apostles don't just sit back. They initiate a plan, which springs from a proper understanding of the problem. Here was an organization failing to cope with increasing demands being made upon it, not a personal ministry failing on the apostles' part or a moral weakness in those making the complaints. Here, at the beginning of the life of the church, the Holy Spirit is giving us all the equivalent of a Jethro insight.

Note that they *initiate* the plan – they don't delegate it. They don't throw their hands up in horror and say, 'That's a management job; we are the speakers.' No, they come up with a management solution that starts with proper diagnosis. They need to get better organized. They need to recognize specialists for certain roles and delegate responsibilities for the completion of the task. Anyone who has ever led a church through growth will know that this is a key transition phase. What once could be done by any and many now needs to be done by some and few, leaving others to focus on what they alone can do.

Fascinatingly, in 1 Peter 4:7–11, Peter reflects this balanced understanding and wise practical outworking:

> The end of all things is near. Therefore be clear minded and self-controlled so that you can pray. Above all, love each other deeply, because love covers over a multitude of sins. Offer hospitality to one another without grumbling. Each one should use whatever gift he has received to serve others, as faithfully administering God's grace in its various forms. If anyone speaks, he should do it as one speaking the very words of God. If anyone serves, he should do it with the strength God provides, so that in all things God may be praised through Jesus Christ. To him be the glory and the power for ever and ever. Amen.

Peter describes both what all Christians should do: pray, love and be hospitable, and then mentions what some are gifted and called to do: speak and serve, the very things being organized here. Both are 'administrations of the grace of God', but in different forms, neither one superior to the other. All are to be 'stewards' discharging a responsibility the Master has entrusted to them as a gift. Note too that personal hospitality is an 'every-Christian grace', not a 'some-Christian gift'. It is to be offered 'without grumbling' (the same as the word used in Acts 6:1; Peter hadn't forgotten the experience of a near train-wreck). Our hospitality, even just a cup of cold water, evidences whether we are a follower of Christ or not. Its active presence shows whether we have believed the gospel or not. In Matthew 25:31–46, the parable of the sheep and the goats most powerfully presents this to us. Hospitality to people who are not like you isn't a given, even in a hospitable culture; it requires grace and intentionality.

Organizing well

What the apostles are doing here then is, in effect, organizing corporate hospitality. They are not neglecting their own personal responsibility to be hospitable, as in this all Christians are required to be involved, and leaders should excel (see 1 Timothy 3:2; Titus 1:8). 'Corporate hospitality' has a different ring about it today, but it's significant, as with many good things, that Christianity came up with it. It's just that in our corporate hospitality, we Christians, rather than buttering up those who might return the favour, help those who can't (see Matthew 5:46–48; Luke 6:32–36; 14:12–14).

The apostles brilliantly gained congregational ownership. Here too is a leadership danger zone. So often a leadership works it all out and announces a decision by decree, and the congregation feels as if they are just pawns in the leaders' grand schemes. The apostles avoided this trap. They led *and* consulted at the same time. The problem was identified by them, and the plan to solve it was announced by them, but they did this in the hearing of all. They convened a special meeting (verse 2), then shared a way forward and gained ownership by involvement and participation.

I don't think that a prescriptive and mandatory pattern is given to us here, but it is suggestive of good practice, what leadership wisdom looks like in action. Why not include everyone when you can? Wise leadership knows what it must and can alone do, but also knows when to involve all and how to do that well. 'Brothers' – that lovely 'we-are-all-family-together' phrase – 'you choose.' This is not a free-for-all. They set up wise criteria and give guidance. They are not control freaks, but show trust and respect for the whole body of Christ. Wisdom does not dwell with them alone.

The solution involved setting apart a small team, chosen by all, whom they empowered to ensure that the vital task was completed. All were now stakeholders. 'This proposal pleased the whole group' (verse 5). The men they chose, all with Greek-background names, would have helped everyone to know things were being done 'in a fitting and orderly way' (1 Corinthians 14:40), and also fostered a real sense that everyone wanted to overcome any perceived grievances.

The team was then publicly set apart: 'They presented these men to the apostles, who prayed and laid their hands on them' (verse 6). All could see who had been empowered to carry out the task. Although the phrase 'we will hand this responsibility over to them' (verse 3b) indicates delegation, I like the term empowerment so much more, and here we see that being outworked.

Performance

Luke significantly calls attention to the result: 'So the word of God spread' (verse 7a). If the church turns in on itself because of conflict or confusion, the greatest danger is that God's Word will get chained up. By keeping cool heads and having courageous hearts, the leaders' actions meant the Word was released to do its work. This is key.

For as this is happening, the church grows in *quantity*: 'The number of disciples in Jerusalem increased rapidly' (verse 7b) and, I believe, in *quality* too (even the priests are getting converted – a 'large number'). When religious professionals are touched by the gospel, a powerful work of God is happening, and Luke wants us to know that this results from the leadership handling an Acts 6 problem brilliantly. We don't hear more about hungry widows and church splits, as these have been dealt with.

Quite a result – and all described in seven verses!

Pointers

There are many lessons here for the contemporary church. As churches grow, they must be very careful not to be deflected from the gospel priority. So much can preoccupy us. Changes in group dynamics are some of the most surprising reasons for the gospel being impeded. It is not enough to abdicate leadership responsibilities and leave issues for someone else to sort out.

Growth and complexity of tasks in church life took the early church leaders by surprise, but they managed their way through it exceedingly well. This story in Acts could also be quoted in management books today.

Notice, very significantly, that the leaders didn't directly employ either of their two main giftings/callings. They could have called for a week of special prayer; they could have started a series of sermons on the need for contentment or the dangers of divisiveness. Yet they didn't. The lesson? Some problems in a growing church can't be fixed by 'just' praying or preaching. They have to be managed, organized and worked through – with courage and skill. Don't use Acts 6 as a reason to retreat to the study to pray and prepare sermons, while neglecting the kinds of problems that can ruin a church. And never underestimate the damage this kind of behaviour can cause, for without a clear awareness of how similar problems can deflect the church from spreading the Word, the momentum of outreach can stall.

Great leadership in action

Leaders are largely untrained in dealing with growing churches, so that when growth happens, they find themselves sucked into contemporary equivalents of sorting out hungry widows but not knowing how to do so effectively. I have talked to many leaders who felt they were fighting pastoral fires, not training leaders or structuring staff so that the gospel could keep going forwards. In the face of many urgent demands, energy and courage to promote gospel growth drained away.

If the insights into church leadership (prophet, priest and king in chapter 2) are right, then this is about gaining some more kingly abilities.

So we can start by implementing James's encouragement to pray for wisdom, with its echoes of Solomon's request for help to lead well. Whereas then it was the sovereign Lord who approached the new king, Solomon, in a dream and gave him the opportunity to ask for whatever he liked, and his request for wisdom pleased the Lord (1 Kings 3:10), now all of us have that privilege. James exhorts, 'If *any of you* lacks wisdom, he should ask God, who gives generously to all without finding fault, and it will be given to him' (James 1:5, emphasis added). What an encouragement to draw on resources so that we can effectively lead 'this great people' who belong to God today.

Great leadership is, as we've seen, about character and skills combined. Character comes first; skills can be picked up. In his seminal book, *Good to Great*, Jim Collins, writing as a not-yet-Christian in a secular context, nevertheless picks up on this when analysing what makes companies 'great'. He and his team used a host of methods to quantify and analyse this, rather than depending on the vagaries of anecdotal evidence. When it came to leadership, he described the now-famous five levels:

- Level 1: 'a highly capable individual';
- Level 2: 'a contributing team member';
- Level 3: 'a competent manager';
- Level 4: 'an effective leader'; and
- Level 5: 'an executive'.

What marked this last level out was a combination of will *and* humility, an ambition for the company to achieve its long-term mission: 'setting up successors for success' (read 2 Timothy 2:2, or more importantly John 20:22 and Acts 1:4–5), combined with a compelling modesty. 'In contrast to other very I-centric style of comparison leaders, we were stuck by how the good-to-great leaders didn't talk about themselves.'[5] Professional determination combines with personal humility to have 'an unwavering resolve to do what must be done' (Acts 6 again).

Collins later described in these moving terms one of the Level 5 leaders he uncovered:

Shortly before his death, I had the opportunity to meet Dave
Packard [co-founder of Hewlett Packard the famous computer
company]. Despite being one of Silicon Valley's first self-made
billionaires, he lived in the same small house that he and his wife
built for themselves in 1957, overlooking a simple orchard. The
tiny kitchen, with its dated linoleum, and the simply furnished
living room bespoke a man who needed no material symbols to
proclaim 'I'm a billionaire. I'm important. I'm successful.' 'His
idea of a good time,' said Bill Terry, who worked with Packard
for thirty-six years, 'was to get some friends together to string
some barbed wire.' Packard bequeathed his $5.6 billion estate
to a charitable foundation and, upon his death, his family crafted
a eulogy pamphlet, with a photo of him sitting on a tractor in
farming clothes. The caption made no reference to his stature as
one of the great industrialists of the twentieth century. It simply
read: 'David Packard, 1912–1996, Rancher, etc.' Level 5, indeed.[6]

Character and capability combined. Surely that is something
that Christian leaders, empowered by the grace of the Spirit
and in imitation of the greatest Servant Leader of all, should
aspire to and live out.

The Acts 6 passage also illustrates the great wisdom
of setting up teams to solve problems and minister practical
compassion. It is notable that the New Testament more
generally points to leadership teams for local churches ('elders'
always being plural in the New Testament church context).
(This is something I will look at in more detail later.)

Being part of the growing church

David Gooding, a former professor of Greek, has argued that
Acts is organized around its growth phases.[7]

Church life in Acts is like white-water rafting – a gentle phase of meanders before you storm into a series of rapids where so much is out of your control (but under God's control). Leaders try to keep things afloat, but God is building his church in the power of his Spirit as the gospel of his Son comes to new territory. Luke marks this at each juncture when the church has a period of getting its breath back (Gooding's key passages). Leaders don't mastermind all of this; God does. Courageously steering their way through the rapids confronting the church is what leaders are called to do. Along the way, they also help the members make the most of opportunities (see Acts 8:14; 11:19–21; Colossians 4:5).

No-one size is endorsed as the ideal or the target at which to aim. That should free us from any sort of one-size-fits-all mentality. But Acts reminds us that living things grow, and those indwelt by the Holy Spirit, alive with the life of God in the soul of man, should be no different.

In this chapter, we have seen the early church face a potentially destabilizing problem which arose in a most surprising way as the church was successfully growing. Let's now move on to help leaders and members steer their way through some of the exciting, but sometimes rough, stuff of church life.

Discussion questions

1. Some key leadership lessons may have stood out in this chapter. What are the ones your church needs to learn and act on? How can you overcome some of the complaints you are aware of? What action points can you implement to free up the gospel?

2. Why may the type of satanic attacks in Acts 6 be neglected by churches and their leaders? How are such pressures raising themselves in your church?

3. Many churches will struggle to identify with the early church's rapid growth and its ability to set up teams of people to carry out tasks – most don't have enough gifted people around. But how might a small church still use the insights from Acts 6?

4. If you are in leadership, how do you set your priorities? Do you take control of your diary, or does the urgent/non-important always win out over the important/non-urgent? Take a look at your 'time/task' allocation as a leadership team. What does this say about your priorities and effectiveness?

4. OVERCOME THREE PRACTICAL LIMITS: ATTENDANCE, BUILDINGS AND CASH

Steve Tibbert tells the story of a London church growing from about 250 people to over 1,000.[1] He highlighted three practical challenges: people, facilities and finance, or as one leader put it: 'ABC – attendance, buildings and cash'. As churches grow, these three factors act as brakes to continued expansion if they are not handled well.

Attendance

We've seen that, as numbers increase, issues start arising. One of the first practical challenges is personnel. As attendance grows, organizing and facilitating the growing workload is beyond even the most well-meaning of volunteers. The single worker of a small-to-medium-sized church will usually do extra work, as well as carry out priority responsibilities. For example, there will be a lot of routine designing, planning and administration. This gradually grows, until the worker could be using 30% of his or her time merely running things. The response to an increased workload is to work faster, but to cope properly, the church will need to hire other people. To raise the finances for this seems a big jump.

I missed a trick for many years. I was always looking for another pastor-teacher to do the same job as me. Then it dawned on me that we could also think laterally and hire people who could do jobs better than me. Administration was one big area, and alongside it went getting a proper church office. Part-time staff were recruited to do community work and did it effectively. Women workers helped with the pastoral workload of our growing church: women whose husbands and partners were not yet believers, single mums, widows, divorcees, those from backgrounds of domestic violence, those with serious relationship issues, and so on. No male pastor in his right mind would take on that kind of workload alone for, even partnering with his wife to counsel those kinds of needs and even working fast, it can be beyond anyone. (Remember Paul's admonition to Titus: '. . . teach the older women . . . Then they can train the younger women' [Titus 2:3–4].)

A leadership team also has the serious task of passing on the baton to the next generation (2 Timothy 2). Why? Our time goes so fast that, before we know it, demographics mean we have become an ageing congregation. To counter this, you may, like Paul with Timothy, take some wise risks by encouraging younger people (see Acts 16:1–3). You may want to 'platform' young adults in meetings and bring them into positions of responsibility. This shows that you have confidence in them and the church has a long-term vision of its future.

Should you import staff or develop 'home-grown'? The former is certainly not wrong; Barnabas went and got Saul from Tarsus to help him in Antioch (Acts 11:25), and Paul took workers with him on his travels (for example, Acts 16:1–5). Maybe the equivalent of this is to provide extra mentoring to those finishing at Bible colleges before they go into ministry or offer apprenticeships to young people to expose them to church life? Talent in your church could be released by a part-time or full-time appointment. The benefit of using people from within is that they know the church already, and you know them. The downside is that developing a proper professional relationship while still being friends with those you serve and have known for ages can be daunting.

Staff need caring for and organizing. Job descriptions, contracts, pay scales, appraisals, disciplinary procedures, pastoral support, legal requirements, deploying and directing all need to be addressed. Many leaders aren't trained in these vital areas or see them as distractions. If the church is to grow, however, these issues will need our attention.

Where people live and how news spreads

Growing attendance brings with it other unanticipated developments. One would hope that the membership would reflect the diversity of people the gospel can reach, geographically as well as sociologically. This may well affect a church's decision to church plant rather than grow larger.

What do I mean by this? Most church plants emphasize immediate locality (we did – our first church plant was based on a walking-distance interpretation of what local meant). Some communities are very localized still.[2]

For most people today, however, geography, community and networks are much more than walking distance. We live in a complex world where geography works at different levels. The seminal work on innovation diffusion emphasized two factors that affect any innovation spreading into a community.[3] There is the spatial factor (nearest distance) *and* the hierarchical factor (innovations usually spread from largest to smallest, down an urban hierarchy). These two work at the same time, sometimes with each other, sometimes in opposition. Typically, an item of news will reach Manchester from London before it spreads to a spatially nearer village in rural Bedfordshire. It's how things diffuse. It's a bit like gravity – big places 'pull' stuff towards them because of the complex web of human relationships, well before the friction of local distance has been overcome.

I knew of a woman who worked on the till of a large store who was expecting a baby. News got around the staff quite quickly. The people she met went home at the end of their shift or after shopping, taking the news with them and passing it on. It spread over a wide area, reaching some people far away much more quickly than those locals at the end of her street. In time it reached those near at hand by a process of relational contact. Networks are not simply distance-defined, but a sophisticated web created by shared values, interests, meetings, technology, ethnicity, cultural mores and other factors.

That's why Paul could write to relatively new churches and say to them, 'The Lord's message rang out from you not only in Macedonia [northern Greece] and Achaia [southern Greece] – your faith in God has become known everywhere' (1 Thessalonians 1:8), for the various links they had with traders and passers-by meant the news spread far and wide. Of Paul's time in Ephesus, a great trading centre, Luke records, '[he] had discussions daily in the lecture hall of Tyrannus. This went on for two years, so that all the Jews and Greeks who lived in the province of Asia heard the word of the Lord' (Acts 19:9–10). There is more going on here than 'nearest-neighbour contagion', but it reflects the geographically dispersed connections people had with a vast hinterland.

Implications

As church attendance grows, networks change.

My wife and I live in a part of Bedford termed 'an area of social deprivation', so we know what local geography looks like in a poor part of a large town.[4] When our children were young, we did much that was very local: mums and toddlers, schools and clubs, for example, and we met many people, some of whom became Christians. As the children got older, their schools were further away. We met different people who lived at a distance. We still invited them to things, and some of them became Christians. New converts will initially go where their friends are. It may take several years of maturing before they are ready to go to a nearer church.

I play sport locally, and the hockey centre is within walking distance of my home. But it casts its net wide: guys come from a 15-mile radius to play and they are my friends. I'd love to help them to faith in Christ. If they did convert, I would love them to be at our church – I have been 'playing, praying and saying' (as the Christians in Sport maxim goes) for twenty years with and for them. That's how networks develop over time. A larger church has a large geographical reach: its networks are complex and will only become more so as people convert. As you age, even in a tight-knit community like mine, friendship circles will change and widen. Advanced old age will mean that personal networks then contract. The church needs to know how to help with this change too.

Friction of distance is a slippery concept. It isn't just measured in physical distance, but also by 'cost' in terms of time, effort and difficulty. Obviously, this 'cost' of travel is far less than it once was. When revival broke out in the small village of Everton in Bedfordshire under the preaching of John Berridge in the eighteenth century, people walked a couple of hours or more to hear the good news. That journey is now possible in about ten minutes.[5]

Usually, small churches envisage local people being converted through local outreach. That's great, and a neighbourhood church may thrive in its restricted area. Yet sometimes the small charge the large with arrogance because of their size and apparent ignoring of the distance factor, when it's really more about geography working at different scales and the outworking of a complex network of relationships. A larger church cannot usually help having a more-than-walking-distance spatial component to its attendance, due to the different impacts of various outreach strategies.

Later, I will describe three outreach strategies churches can employ, but it is worth reflecting now on their impact on the geography of the local church.

Geography and types of local-church evangelism

Firstly, a 'Come and See' strategy, in which friends are invited to events, has a spatial limit which is different from when you ask, 'How far would I be prepared to travel to church?' These friends will not be prepared to travel as far as you are. In short, if your invitation involves extensive travel, it becomes much harder for them to attend. If you build up a network from where you live, and if that is a long way from where you worship with other believers, you are making it very difficult for others to come to events. So, to tie in with any effective Come and See that your church organizes may require a radical look at where you live.

Secondly, the 'Care and Serve' strategy, where good deeds touch people's lives, works well at local community level. It works best where relationships are being made via the Deed ministry of the church, and not just formally at some kind of 'service outlet', but also informally through bumping into church people at schools, local shops and community forums. Choosing to live nearer to be accessible to others in the community helps take this forward.

Thirdly, 'Go and Tell' as a strategy can involve sharing the gospel with those either near at hand or miles away. Believers may get opportunities to share their faith with colleagues. Given the pattern of commuting, this may extend the geographical reach of a church, or it may mean partnering with other churches nearer to where the person lives. Some might develop friendships at a distant leisure activity and then lead someone to Christ in that context. It will take wisdom to guide the new convert as to which church they should attend.

If growth happens in all three strategy areas, the church will not only grow numerically but also spread geographically. That may not be a problem if all can get to church, bring their friends and serve the community. Typically, however, some may be travelling quite a way. The church may need to extend the scope of the gospel by planting a new congregation in another place. This can be an excellent way to get the gospel out to people further away.

Buildings

Some small churches continue to meet in homes, although I know very few in the UK maintaining this for very long. Sooner or later, a public building will be used. This brings all sorts of issues to light, number one being *limitation*. The size of a building will affect such things as your church's vision, its willingness to take risks to reach other people, its financial ability to underwrite serious community compassion ministry and its ability to pay for a growing staff base. Most of all, you will be affected by the 80% rule: when it's about 80% full, it will feel completely full. You may get a few more people in sometimes, but you will plateau.

We did. Our church has hired buildings for the whole of its forty-year history. We moved numerous times to larger venues when necessary. As we got larger, it became more difficult to find suitable premises. Once, when we were 80% full in a hall, we stopped growing for about four years. We changed building, gained more space, and growth began once again. I am not intending to be simplistic, but space can be a limiting factor, affecting people's vision and expectations of growth.

Think carefully about alternatives to bigger buildings

'Church plant, then,' I hear you say. We did – in fact we attempted four plants, two successfully. This seems to over-come the building limitation problem. Yet some clear thinking is needed, so that when churches plant, they are aware of a host of factors and don't do it just to avoid a building issue or presumed financial pressures.

Four factors to consider

Firstly, the theory 'plant churches which church plant' reads well. But in practice? Interestingly, the Charismatic House-church Movement of the late 1970s and 1980s points to a way forward for that type of church-growth. Many of them went on to either (a) become larger and growing, operating as a large church with small groups, or (b) fold, for a variety of reasons: leaderships taking a few followers into wacky pathways, overly heavy shepherding to try to keep the group afloat or just a wearing down due to a lack of growth. After twenty or so years of the experiment, most of the house churches of that period became the same kinds of organiza-tions as other church streams, facing similar challenges of growth and complexity.

Secondly, most churches plant, using the 'strawberry model' of taking a 'sucker' off the main church and establishing it nearby. Usually, some members in the area, perhaps in an existing house group, are encouraged to see themselves as the nucleus of the new church and urged to go forward. Support, finance and perhaps personnel are provided by the mother church. This can be a very positive way to church plant. Yet it has its geographical limitations in that the plant will be in the same general geographical area and not in a needy town 50 miles away. If many plants are done using this method, it can lead to a concentration of churches in one area. If you planted regularly like that in a medium-sized town or small city, you would soon have many small church plants close to one another, all duplicating ministry and costing a lot to sustain.

Another method is to 'parachute in' some workers and volunteers to a place many miles away. After a couple of attempts at strawberry plants, we seriously looked into this, noting where people were and where gospel churches weren't. Putting very small groups into plants like this is slow going. Necessary, but also very tough.

Churches cooperating may overcome some of the big hurdles to planting in difficult places. With three other gospel churches, we are involved in doing this in a large town near to us, investing significant finances and personnel into supporting a fledgling work. None of the churches could have done it singly, but together we can achieve something substantial.

Thirdly, in a rapidly growing church, planting may not solve the numbers problem. A fast-growing church could grow at around 10% a year. Taking out a typical church-planting group of around thirty people to start one, you would need to do that each and every year to solve the problem of too many people and not enough space in a large church of over 300.

You would have to find good leaders (often the issue determining success . . . or not!) and fund them (given that most church plants take a few years to self-fund).

Finally, one of the main issues to think about is not the first ten years of a church plant, but what happens when churches grow and start to level off, once the initial vision is realized. One senior leader's observation was that many church plants of the 1980s and 1990s had plateaued, and his conviction was we need to train leaders to keep churches growing into larger size brackets, rather than growing lots of small ones which stall.

It's easy to forget, even as church planters move on from one plant to the next, that the people they leave behind require a plan too, that is: 'Here's what you do with the rest of your Christian and church life.' People need a vision that will help them to keep moving forward.

Principled pragmatism

So what's the alternative to a church growing and the building becoming a constraint?

I had serious theological objections to anything other than 'at least one meeting a week where all the disciples gather to express their fundamental unity and where they take one loaf and one cup'. However, through hearing about a comment from the eminent Bible teacher, Don Carson, I have been helped here. He argued that if nothing could be done about the church's building and the church was seeing gospel blessing, it should go for 'principled pragmatism'. That is to say, steps are taken to make sure that the gospel keeps succeeding until the building problem can be solved. For many, this will mean considering multiple services.

After a long consultation, we went for two meetings back-to-back in the same morning, which has enabled the church to keep growing in the largish building we hire until we can come up with another solution.

Others try multi-site. We tried that (separate mornings and/or evenings in different buildings), but found it less satisfactory compared to multi-servicing in one building. New people who go to a different site will inevitably identify with that part of the church and it becomes 'total church' for them; that is, they will feel the congregation they attend is 'their church', and they will not easily identify with other congregations who share the same name or who are in the same organization. Multi-site is church planting by another route – fine, but it is worth being candid that this happens, rather than thinking that a multi-site set-up can indefinitely continue to be part of one church organization led by one leadership. Some US mega-churches (and some smaller UK ones) are trying to overcome this by using video technology to enable multi-campuses to still see and hear the same Bible teacher. Is the jury still out on the long-term effects of this? I think so.

Plan carefully

Multi-service needs careful consideration. Get it wrong and you will have two competing congregations, or, worse still, the once forward-moving large gathering will stall badly as the church goes backwards into something not even attractive or energetic. Not enough thought about who will do what means a few do a lot (again), get worn down, and it all becomes unsustainable.

Before we had multiple morning services, we learned from what others had found out the hard way. One church scheduled the same musicians to do the whole morning (getting there before 8am and arriving home way after 1pm). It worked fine for a short time while people were enthusiastic, but, as it became a regular feature, frustrations increased and the church eventually had to go back to a one-meeting format. Other churches misjudged in that when they transitioned to two meetings, they found that nearly everyone chose the same one and there was not a good spread over both. When we polled our members, we discovered that opting for 9am and 11am (so much neater for publicity) would have meant that nearly everyone would have gone for 11am. Alternatively, 9.30am and 11.30am meant that very few wanted the late second service. So we ended up with a rather unusual 9.15 and 11.15 format, offering a good numerical balance over both. We also have a 6pm service which helps shift workers, outsiders and single people. Your solution may look very different.

Sustainability is key for multiple services, so we don't require anyone to stay for both, apart from the service leader and the preacher. Everything is done by new teams – greeting, coffee, crèche, music, set-up, prayers, Bible readings, the lot. No-one becomes worn down.

We took over a year to talk it over, get all on board and discuss practicalities with the teams that make Sunday happen, then planned for a launch.[6] It felt really weird for a while, but we have got used to it. It has facilitated further growth, and we have longer-term capacity to grow in the same building.

Continued growth, however, will lead to pressure to do something about the building. You may be facing this issue too. The 'go-and-get-a-bigger-building' approach has its lessons too. I have visited many church building projects and seen the good, the bad and the more-than-ugly. I have heard of wasted time and money, poorly thought-through plans, and auditoria built far too small but at great cost. If your church is being held up by facilities, read up on it, learn as much as you can from others and seek God for what is possible in your location so that the gospel is not held up.[7]

Money, money, money

The final practical issue that will hold things up is finances. Partly, this has to do with the type of converts that your church might win. Affluent converts, like Lydia in Acts 16:15, may be great in this context, but needy young women will not be (see Acts 16:16–17). If your church does a lot of successful community work, you may have quite a few of the latter – and you can praise God you know the joy of 1 Corinthians 1:26–27: 'Not many of you were . . . but God chose . . .' This kind of growth is sometimes missing from conservative evangelical churches, perhaps because of the lack of both Deed ministry and cultural adaptation to people unlike us. Such growth means that fewer people can contribute to the staff costs – just at a time when you need *extra* staff to help organize people to serve both the church and the community. The gap between what is needed to take ministry forward effectively and what is likely to flow in from a group of people, many of whom don't earn much money, can become a serious problem. The affluent will have to become much more sacrificial with the resources God has entrusted to them.

In small-to-medium-sized churches, people often give in response to arising, immediate needs. But there has to be funding available for the long-term development of other workers too, and establishing a training fund will be a good way to promote this. Encouraging members to give via legacies to such a fund will strengthen the long-term commitment of the whole church to training. But transitioning from a short-term to a longer-term budget is never an easy phase for a church to grow through.

Staff cost money; equipment costs money; buildings cost money; and improving the aesthetics isn't cheap either. Helping in the community is definitely resource-demanding, as is supporting mission and compassion ministries at home and overseas. With all these requirements, money is always going to be scarce and has to be carefully marshalled (see 1 Timothy 5 – 6).

Churches may be more resource-hungry than we realize. So what's the cost?

One church plant grew to about eighty. They hired buildings, worked hard and fifteen years later, they looked at their figures again. They still had about eighty, though not exactly the same people as there had been a lot of change (for reasons such as ageing/dying, people moving in and out, people leaving for university). Over that whole period, the financial expenditure had been in the order of £1.5 million. That's a high resource demand to keep a church going, once it has gone beyond its initial growth spurt.

Now, that isn't at all a reason for *not* planting, but it is worth pondering. If you planted several churches, and they all grew to around that size for that length of time, the real financial cost would be much higher than most people realize. One can take a deep gasp at the cost of a building project, without realizing that any alternative *also* has a cost. It may not be much less, and arguably even higher, than the cost of the large building.

Room for a 10% improvement?
Is the situation in the UK worse because so few Christians take tithing to their church seriously? I am not saying that people don't give, but giving to other Christian organizations tends to be high up on the list, and the local church may receive what is left over. Many newer churches emphasize tithing more candidly, clearly understanding that unless generosity of this nature is a reality, the work of the gospel and the growth of the church will be hindered.

On top of all that, the funding of a major building project may mean that a large church faces a need to raise massive amounts of money. Many pastors struggle with this challenge. Indeed, it can be tempting to wish it would go away – it seems it ought to go into someone else's in-tray. Yet the apostle Paul invested significant time and effort in fund-raising, in his case for the relief of the poor in Jerusalem. He saw it as a witness to the church's oneness and the gospel's effectiveness. Clearly it was a heavy burden, but he didn't shirk it (see 2 Corinthians 8 – 9). Notice the seriousness with which he took it:

> [H]e was chosen by the churches to accompany us as we carry the offering, which we administer in order to honour the Lord himself and to show our eagerness to help. We want to avoid any criticism of the way we administer this liberal gift. For we are taking pains to do what is right, not only in the eyes of the Lord but also in the eyes of men.
>
> (2 Corinthians 8:19–21)

Many a pastor will have to get his fundraising jacket on, and help the people of God to give sacrificially to a gospel cause. For the key point surely is that people are not giving to a building fund but giving to gospel success in the future. Only believing the gospel deeply will encourage the kind of giving that makes a difference.

Leading through practical challenges

So then, three huge issues affect the success or otherwise of the gospel. Church leaders can't ignore them or say, 'They are not part of the ministry.'

To cope with just those three practical realities (let alone the myriad of other things), leadership teams will inevitably have to do a lot of praying and deliberating. They may need to get external advice (recall Barnabas and Paul in Acts 11:25), intentionally invest significant resources into their own training, carefully monitor the church's and staff's workload and think ahead about future requirements. They will need to carve out adequate time to reflect on all of this; it can't be done in a hurry, for the repercussions of decisions in these three zones will *last a long time* – for good or for ill.

Meanwhile, shepherd leaders must recall what the sheep are doing while all of this goes on. Sheep look at the grass before their nose. If it's there, they are happy. Shepherds, however, have to assess the amount of pasture left and often decide to move the flock on, well before the sheep are ready. The sheep will often bleat (loudly) at changes necessary to keep a church growing in effectiveness. You must realize that you are Mr Under-shepherd (1 Peter 5:2–6), and get on with the job.

Discussion questions

1. What are your 'pinch points' at the moment: not the right staff, too small a building, not enough money? All three perhaps, but which is the dominant problem stopping you growing?
2. Have you ever had an outsider come and audit your building for its helpfulness in enabling outsiders to access what goes on in it? What positives might a makeover offer?
3. Your financial accounts may get examined each year, but do you look at them properly? Is there a discussed budget? Could savings be made to redirect resources elsewhere? Does the church's income reflect the wealth of its members or is there room for improvement? Discuss wise ways to take all this forward.
4. Is the church seeking God to guide it to future workers? The fields are white for harvest; people need reaching with the gospel; churches need to be planted and grown. Such initiatives are people-led more than money- or building-led. Is this a priority prayer issue in your leadership times together?

5. RISE TO THE CHALLENGE: HANDLING MULTIPLE RESPONSIBILITIES

Multi-tasking is something that men (apparently being from Mars) are not supposed to be able to do very well, especially as they contemplate the problems of church growth isolated in their caves (aka pastor's / vicar's study).[1] It is tempting to say, 'Just leave me alone to pray and preach.' But multi-task you must if you are a church leader, for shepherding the flock is a multi-task calling. You have to protect, feed, nurture, lead, comfort, exhort, bear with, teach, rebuke, correct, model, organize and plan. Lots of things to do at the same time.

Learning from others

A few years ago, the British medical fraternity published research on what helped doctors make progress, after their surgeries were audited and they were given feedback on their personal practice. Patient feedback only went so far; it could be flatteringly complimentary or seethingly critical. External expert consultant audits didn't necessarily help either. Everyone would smarten up their act while they were around, but results weren't long-lasting. What did help, however, was feedback *from fellow practitioners*. When GPs from other practices discussed what could be improved, and shared changes their own surgeries had implemented, they found doctors much more willing to listen. Change was now longer-lasting.[2]

Pastors also learn best from fellow practitioners. Though we should be rightly wary of cut-and-paste or plug-and-play approaches to church ministry, borrowing good ideas, wise structures and best practice from other churches and leaders can indeed help take the work forward.

A mental map for church leaders

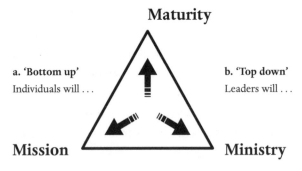

Figure 5.1: Maturity, Ministry and Mission

To help with multiple responsibilities, some leaders have come up with mental maps of what the church and its leadership need to concentrate on.[3] Above is one that is particularly useful for small through to awkward-sized churches. It takes common themes from others, but stresses the need to work at areas of the Christian life *simultaneously*. It offers wise advice reflecting scriptural emphases. However, it is definitely not a methodological shortcut to success. It comes from a practical perspective, focusing on how to overcome blockages. It's not a globalizing diagram, but helps a leadership focus on specific key areas.

Going in the right direction

Now, why have a mental map at all? Why not just preach the Bible and see what happens? Fine, but even then you will have an organizing principle in your head. Will you start at the beginning and just work through or will you balance Old and New Testaments? Will you balance Gospels with Epistles? How long will it take you? A senior minister I know covers the whole Bible in ten years. I found that a useful practice and I am now on my third time round. But I'm unsure that it's a scheme that balances the many things that need teaching in the life of a church, let alone the many practical things that need organizing.

Organizations spend time, money and energy on tasks, meetings, people and systems. How do you know if these are out of kilter? Is a dominant person requesting too many resources to be poured into a pet project? Where should the next staff appointment be? Is discipleship being neglected because of all the other activities? Are members getting enough training to share their faith, or has the leadership subtly fallen into the trap of thinking that because people hear lots of biblical material, it automatically translates into action? Who is answerable to whom, and where does the reporting of bad news go? What's the decision-making cascade and authority hierarchy? These are all significant organizational questions.

Some decisions will be intuitive, others will be policy state-
ments agreed by the group; some will be 'just the way we do
it round here', others will be directed by biblical commands.
Many leaders get into such a whirl of busyness that they can't
see the wood for the trees. The urgent takes over from the
important, and how do you know what the important is
anyway?

This is all so much more so when churches transition into
other size categories. Usually growth comes gradually, so it
can be hard to see that life is changing and will need organizing in different ways. Without some kind of directional
guidance it can be hard to know where to steer next, what
aspects of the group's life need extra resourcing and where to
direct the limited leadership time and energy.

I say mental map (I was a geographer), but for you it may
be a flow chart, a spider diagram, an accountability chart, an
organization diagram, a vision matrix or a responsibility list.
It helps to have something giving you a sense you are pulling
in the right direction and reflecting the Bible's teaching. Or,
as US church leader Rick Warren would say, *its* purposes
rather than *your own*.

The Barnabas factor

A good example of getting this right in action is Barnabas in
Acts 11:

> He was a good man, full of the Holy Spirit and faith, and a great
> number of people were brought to the Lord. Then Barnabas
> went to Tarsus to look for Saul, and when he found him, he
> brought him to Antioch. So for a whole year Barnabas and Saul
> met with the church and taught great numbers of people. The
> disciples were called Christians first at Antioch.
>
> (Acts 11:24–26)

The gospel was having a huge effect (mission), and there was some teaching. But Barnabas realized it wasn't enough. He needed to help the new converts to grow spiritually (maturity). Not many of us would go and get a Bible preacher of superior ability to supplement our own teaching. Remember it wasn't long before it became Paul and Barnabas and not the way round it is here. Barnabas realized that the need of the hour was to see converts becoming disciples, which was what they are called by the end of the year after being taught by these two leaders (verse 26).

Interestingly, we then read:

> During this time some prophets came down from Jerusalem to Antioch. One of them, named Agabus, stood up and through the Spirit predicted that a severe famine would spread over the entire Roman world (This happened during the reign of Claudius.) The disciples, each according to his ability, decided to provide help for the brothers living in Judea. This they did, sending their gift to the elders by Barnabas and Saul.
> (Acts 11:27–30)

The disciples are involved in *ministry*. They serve their brothers and sisters very practically indeed. It was a 'service' or 'ministration'. Here the Word prompts the deed (note that connection again and see also 2 Thessalonians 2:16–17). In fact, so important was the deed that the disciples parted with their two main Bible teachers to ensure the gift arrived safely and that unity and fellowship were maintained between the churches.

In this chapter, I am going to describe the main points of the 'map', and then in subsequent chapters take a more detailed look at each area, particularly focusing within three chapters on what may help your church to grow, whatever size it may be.

Individuals and leaders

Implementation of this particular mental map has two elements. First is a 'bottom-up' emphasis where individuals commit to each of the three areas. Each person needs to see how maturity, ministry and mission can develop. It also needs a 'top-down' lead and practical organization, which leaders must facilitate.

Individual ownership

The three goals need *personal ownership*: 'I personally will commit to growing up into maturity to become like Christ, to serving my fellow believers in ministry and to sharing in mission the good news with those who don't yet know him.'

Many leaders challenge, cajole and sometimes even exhort (= shout at?) people to do these things. Yet is no good just doing this. I learned the hard way, especially when we were transitioning. As new people came, they seemed to be added to the fringe. I assumed they weren't committed, but consuming the parts of church they liked. So I would urge more dedication. I am reminded of what Oliver Cromwell did in desperation when he wanted change in Scotland after the battle of Dunbar; he prayed/exhorted out loud for *three hours!*[4]

The key to gaining personal ownership is not so much at habit level (though forming good habits is important), but at heart level. Only believing the gospel deeply can change our desires so that, trusting in and experiencing the grace of God, we will *want* to do those things that please the Lord. The 'affections' direct the will. The power that impels us simultaneously towards each of the three goals is always the gospel and the work of the Spirit in our hearts.

Many preachers make a mistake here. They preach evangelistically to see people converted and then edifyingly to see believers grow in what theologians call sanctification. Most of the content addressed to the latter group is shaped as information for the mind and directions for the will. Of course, these matter: the apostle Paul has lots of imperatives (what to do) after a series of indicatives (what's been done for you and in you by the gospel). But preachers often disconnect these, and what gets heard is a lot of: 'You must try harder!'

I recall my first sabbatical break (after twenty tiring ministry years). Listening to preaching as I visited other gospel churches, what did I find week after week? Yes, you've guessed it, exhortation after exhortation. The emphasis was on being more committed and then people would please God. One Sunday when I was contemplating what I would like to do on Monday – body-boarding in the surf in Cornwall – I was overwhelmed with a message that kept saying, 'Give your best to God.' Obviously I should; that was manifestly a true point. Yet, I wondered how body-boarding during a sabbatical could ever count as doing that? I felt guilty doing almost anything, let alone enjoying the beach.

I also wondered, 'Is this what I do to the people of God who listen to me every week?'

I asked myself, 'Was my heart touched by believing more deeply in the finished work of Christ, or was I mainly subjected to directions to live in a certain way?' Do preachers assume people know the gospel and believe it, and consequently think believers don't need to be shown Christ as the one whose beauty makes their hearts adore him? Is the gospel seen as something for the unsaved only? Of course, once we have believed it, we don't need to be re-justified week after week. But when Luther was quizzed about why he kept emphasizing justification and the work of Christ as much as he did, he reputedly said, 'Because I forget it every day'.

By motivating believers with gospel grace, you will see a greater degree of personal ownership of these three areas of personal discipleship.[5]

Leaders enabling disciples to grow to maturity

The three goals need to be facilitated by the leadership. Let's look first at how leaders may develop maturity. Notice the close connection between Christ giving leaders to his church and the whole church reaching maturity (see Ephesians 4:11–13). Leaders are challenged to 'shepherd the flock' (see Acts 20:28; 1 Peter 5:2). This involves both content and context.

Content

'Feed my sheep' (John 21:17) should be ringing in our ears at this point. Leaders have to be insightful and deliberate here. For there will always be movements and currents of ideas which may mean that 'the whole will of God' (Acts 20:27) might not be covered in a balanced way or that church life merely reflects the newest thing to be embraced (or not!). Paul didn't hesitate to 'preach anything that would be helpful' and made sure that all felt the challenge to 'turn to God in repentance and have faith in our Lord Jesus' (Acts 20:19–20).

'Teach, teach, teach' is the repetition that stands out, as a younger leader is instructed by an apostle (see Titus 2:1, 3, 6, 9, 15). Biblically truthful, faithfully applied and wisely handled teaching is what grows disciples (Titus 3:8–9). 'Milk and meat' have to be served according to the appetite and health of the listeners (1 Corinthians 3:1–2).

'Take care of my sheep' also involves a 'guarding' element (see Acts 20:28–31). The flock needs protection from all that is false and delusional. Some will need a 'sharp rebuke', even as others are given encouragement (Titus 1:13; 2:15b). Some even need 'silencing', because of the damage that false teaching does in 'ruining whole households' (Titus 1:11).

Context

All this is delivered into a variety of teaching formats. Paul talked about teaching 'publicly and from house to house' (Acts 20:20). With leaders, he could say, 'Remember that for three years I never stopped warning each of you night and day with tears' (Acts 20:31). Large-group, small-group, personal, formal and informal settings are all appropriate contexts for Word communication.

But growing disciples is much more. The word 'example' stands out. Disciples need to see, as well as hear, what growing to be Christlike entails. Paul finished his message to a leadership team with these words: 'In everything I did, I showed you that by this kind of hard work we must help the weak, remembering the words the Lord Jesus himself said: "It is more blessed to give than receive"' (Acts 20:35). To another young leader he wrote, 'Set an example for the believers in speech, in life, in love, in faith and in purity' (1 Timothy 4:12). So the teacher is to embody the truth and, as a mentor, is to encourage others. So much so that Paul could say, 'Whatever you have learned or received or heard from me, or *seen in me* – put it into practice' (Philippians 4:9, emphasis added).

Being mentored alongside other believers is vital. Too many of our training schemes involve knowledge transference, but not necessarily the communication of other necessary and important qualities. The American author Jay Adams has a brilliant insight into disciples being 'with' Jesus so that they might be 'like' Jesus (Mark 3:14; Luke 6:40). He pinpoints the proof that this method worked when it was recorded later: 'When they saw the courage [you can't learn that from a book!] of Peter and John and realised that they were unschooled, ordinary men, they were astonished and they took note that these men had been with Jesus' (Acts 4:13).[6]

Structuring growth to maturity is important too. For example, Titus is told to straighten things out. He does this by appointing properly qualified leaders who then protect and provide for the disciples (Titus 1:5–6). Without structuring for adequate leadership to deliver wholesome teaching and set a worthy example, disciples may flounder as 'mere infants' (see the connection between 1 Corinthians 3:1 and 4:17). Other structures may need to be in place to promote growth. Timothy, for instance, is given an action plan to help widows (1 Timothy 5:3–16).

Disciples aren't just grown so that they can serve God at their church's meetings either. 'Whole-life' discipleship is the goal. Leaders need to assess how they are equipping believers to serve God in all of the 168 hours he gives them every week. So, for example, slaves were to 'show that they can be fully trusted, so that in every way they will make the teaching about God our Saviour attractive' (Titus 2:10).

A leadership team will need to give careful thought to all these issues if they are to provide a place where disciples can develop healthily. (We'll look later in more specific detail at fostering a church context in which disciples can grow into maturity.)

Ministry and mission

Ministry: where all are servants
If disciples grow by serving (see John 13:3–17) and not just by gaining more knowledge, how do we develop this? What about your members and their *ministry*? How is that organized in your church?

As a church, we got bogged down here for quite a while. The awkward-size issues described earlier really hit us hard. Then, we slowly began to understand that the leadership wasn't clarifying the *pathways* to involvement, and new people needed more practical guidance. One of the best things we did was run an induction/new members' day explaining to people how the church worked, and not just what it believed. As well as talking about the faith, we needed to guide people into avenues of service. They needed not only to understand our structure, but also to be told how teams worked, what role they could play, to be told *not* to overcommit to too many teams, and how they could try out different teams or transfer between them. This helped engage many more new people.

Mission: the toughest nut to crack

Mission – surely what churches do well? Hmm.

Lots of churches feel pretty defeated in this area. Individual Christians feel failures too. Many see themselves as useless at winning others to the faith, and deep down they doubt if anyone they know will ever become a Christian.

Pastors get frustrated with the lack of success, and faithfulness becomes the watchword instead. Yet should it be 'either mission success by compromising the message or mission stalled but at least we're faithful'?

Another problem is that staff workers will try to persuade church members to give up some of their spare time to fulfil the workers' mission plans for the church. Instead of developing whole-life disciples living for the Lord as full-time Christian workers wherever God has placed them, sharing the faith becomes focused into a spare-time activity for the keen.[7]

Mission, moreover, becomes narrowly focused on what has been called a 'two-chapter gospel', rather than a 'four-chapter gospel'.[8] Instead of a 'creation, fall, redemption, restoration' message, Christians emphasize only the problem of sin and the personal need for forgiveness. They aren't so conscious of the bigger picture which involves the Lord who made the cosmos and gives every good gift, fixing all the problems caused by sin. In the 'four-chapter gospel', in which disciples are aware of *both* the cultural mandate to go and develop the world *and* the hope for a renewed earth at the return of the King, believers are drawn into a much more expansive mission, but which still has the cross of Christ and personal salvation at the centre.

Leaders faced with the challenge of mission can back away into church life and spend virtually all their time looking after Christians. They may still be busy, but are they as productive as they could be? Is the Word getting locked inside a church's four walls and not being released to transform lives because of a sense of missional inadequacy? Are leaders and their churches failing to reach their full redemptive potential?

It's time to zoom in, focus intently and glean as much as we can about each zone of our map. Each area will reveal leadership and discipleship insights that can be harnessed to take your church forward. Together, they will combine, so that you too will be ready to grow.

Discussion questions

1. What are the Strengths, Weaknesses, Opportunities and Threats (SWOT analysis) your church faces? To handle that information and to shape the future direction of the church, have you got plans in place already? Most churches haven't! In all likelihood though, you will have some intuitive sense or half-formulated ideas. So what are they?

2. How can we stop our planning becoming an unchristian injection of human pride and presumption into the purity of all that God has planned for his church?

3. Discuss as leaders and as a church how you allocate resources. Where does most of the money go? Where are most of the volunteer hours focused? What requires the most energy, anxiety or thought? What brings the most joy to you and to members?

4. As an individual, do you feel that you are cajoled or attracted into becoming more like Christ? Which is more dominant in your experience? Why might that be?

5. Ask new people how they initially found involvement in the life of your church. What was clear as crystal, what never got explained and what still confuses them as they try to serve the other members of God's family?

6. Share your fears, failures and disappointments about getting the gospel to other people. How can our plans and schemes become more gospel-shaped? One way to think of it is to ask, 'Should church life be more like a cruise liner or an RNLI lifeboat?' What expectations and goals shape the people on those two very different types of vessels? Which is your church more like?

6. GROW TO MATURITY: HELPING DISCIPLES GROW UP INTO CHRIST

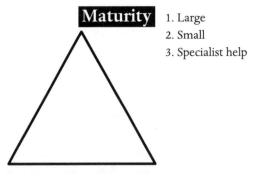

Figure 6.1: Ministry map: focus on Maturity

Hesitatingly, I walked down a dark alleyway on a wet, gloomy night and knocked on the door of a flat whose number had been given to me during a phone call. Apparently, the occupant had mentioned to a Christian organization that he wanted a visit from a church leader. This was the visit and I was the leader, one year in and frighteningly inexperienced. Several knocks later, the door opened a crack. Unshaven, threateningly dressed in a black leather jacket and looking very suspiciously at me, a man said, 'Hello', and allowed me in. I felt very uncomfortable. Then he told me his story.

Martin came from a religious family, but had not taken much interest until in his teens when an older brother had become a real Christian. Taken by his sibling to meetings, he had asked Christ to forgive him. But he hadn't been able to get along to church much, had stalled and then gone backwards. A lack of teaching and encouragement had left him bereft, and life had drifted by him. He had been to university and was about to fail another degree. If not stillborn, here was a believer stuck in a helpless baby phase. Renewed contact with the gospel made him aware that he needed to cry, as infants do, for help. At that moment, I was the help!

Mercifully, God was with the two of us. He brought us both through that nervous initial encounter, so that Martin has become a mature believer and I a maturer leader. I subsequently learned that his unshaven look always develops by ten every morning, even when he close shaves, that the black jacket shouldn't lead me instantaneously to judge another's character, that God can restore his wandering children and, given the right conditions, grow them to wonderful Christlike people who glorify him and attract others to the Saviour.

So when we talk about growing to maturity, it's not theory we have in mind, but lives transformed by the gospel and made beautiful by God's Spirit. Setting the right conditions is important: a lack of them had led Martin to be almost indistinguishable from a non-Christian. Their presence has led to his flourishing, a happy marriage and family life, usefulness in the workplace and service in the church.

So how can leaders and churches practically deliver a format in which this kind of growth can be fostered? I emphasized the importance of teaching earlier and now I want to focus upon the setting for that teaching.

I will be talking mainly about 'gathered church' issues, yet I realize that represents only ten out of the 120 waking hours most disciples can give to church activity. Some leaders put too much pressure on busy people to support activities the church organizes, and often don't give enough support to help disciples in the rest of life. Elsewhere, disciples put their church's meetings very low on their priority list, giving only the leftovers of their time and energy, to the detriment of the corporate Christian experience. The gathered church must facilitate the growth to maturity of the scattered church. This dynamic interplay between 'gathered' and 'scattered' must not be forgotten in any discussion of church size and growth.

Large: growing disciples in growing churches

Early Acts shows the church experiencing life and growth: 'Those who accepted his message were baptised, and about three thousand were added to their number that day. They devoted themselves to the apostles' teaching and to the fellowship, to the breaking of bread and to prayer' (Acts 2:41–42).

Belief, baptism, life, leadership, teaching, fellowship, eating/community life and prayer are descriptors of the church in action, helping its new converts to grow. Some have seen 'two marks' of the church; others three, some (a different) nine.[1] But all are agreed that some kind of Word ministry *to* disciples and service life *for* disciples is a key to seeing believers grow.

To facilitate teaching and service, our church organizes around a strategy of 'large, small and specialist help'. We encourage believers to attend something large: a gathering for worship, edification, teaching and sharing. The early church met as a huge group in the temple courts (Acts 2:46; see also 4:4, 'the number of men grew to about five thousand'; 5:14, 'the Lord . . . added to their number'; and 6:7, 'The number of disciples in Jerusalem increased rapidly'). Some churches had meetings much more limited in size, maybe in the large rooms and courtyards of wealthy members' homes (for example, the 120 of Acts 1:15). Others met in small groups, possibly outdoors (where Lydia first met the gospel, Acts 16:13) or perhaps in more modest homes ('Nympha and the church in her house', Colossians 4:15). It's hard to tell just how big these gatherings were. Households consisted of far much more than our nuclear families and a head of a house might have managed a relatively large group of people, including many dependent relatives, a few visiting cousins, some servants and slaves and many children. Houses for such small clans were much larger than our two-up, two-down terrace (although my gran brought up eleven children in one of those!).

In all these size contexts, believers gathered together for worship and encouragement. Disciples could grow to maturity in any of them. The small shouldn't despise the large or vice versa. But disciples don't grow to maturity in lonely isolation (Ephesians 4:12–13). Meetings matter (see Hebrews 10:25–26).

Maturity, unity and diversity
Though it has been fashionable for a while to espouse the targeting of particular groups for church planting and for-mation (the 'homogenous-unit principle'), the New Testament relishes the intergenerational, interracial and intercultural challenge of reaching and keeping a diverse group of people together. The glue is the gospel, not the socio-economic or shared human-cultural traits that typify other groups. The

church is unlike any other organization, and its diversity-in-unity, as we've seen, is a massive witness to the watching world. In settings where believers have to 'flex' to embrace warmly other believers so unlike them, maturity develops properly.

If the church splinters into groups along age, economic, social, ethnic or other identity markers, its precious unity will be lost. The glue keeping it together will not be the gospel, but a sub-gospel unity. This may be around preferences such as: 'It's our kind of music', 'It's our kind of teaching' or 'It's our class of people'. Without constant attention to this issue, a church can harbour cliques based around merely human characteristics.

Human nature tends to find its security, identity and need for affirmation in something less than the grace of God in the gospel. We look to people to meet these deep drives. We cling to what is 'like me'. And so we must keep making the gospel the basis for meeting people's deepest desires, and learn to grow beyond an immature basis for meeting them.

Glynn Harrison, Emeritus Professor of Psychiatry at the University of Bristol, comments, 'Most growing churches today positively *play* to our culture's preference for informality and individuality.' He mentions authors Jennifer Twenge and Keith Campbell's research into the current epidemic of narcissism, and their view that, 'Today's most successful churches have adapted cleverly to our self-oriented culture by front-ending their appeal to what people want.'[2]

So church can be a less-than-ideal place for spiritual growth to maturity. Yet it needn't be, and many churches aren't like that.

Where do you find security?

Two other barriers to maturity are: (a) where the meetings of the church, especially a large church, become a substitute for the *personal* discipleship life of the leader or the disciple; or (b) where the individual develops a dependent relationship with a mentor and lives out the Christian life through another's closeness to God, as if it were their own. Let's expand on both of those.

Barrier 1: The gathered church on a Sunday can assume more prominence in the leaders' and members' minds than discipleship during the week. This happens partly because the Sunday meetings absorb a lot of thinking as they get bigger. Logistics, organization, planning and preparation, and all at so many levels, are invested into making Sunday work.

It is easy to slip into thinking, 'This is the spiritual part of my life which God is really interested in.' We subtly take on board a sacred/secular mindset. Leaders and preachers invest energy into ensuring that the church has God-honouring meetings. They then tend to focus on getting members to support all their attempts at numerical and spiritual growth via the meetings. The implication is that growth is all about attending meetings.

Members too may be buoyed up by Sundays and in danger of seeing meetings as the place where they feel safe and where real worship happens, to the neglect of their whole-life worship (Romans 12:1–3). Instead of meetings leading to maturity, they keep believers somewhat infantile and dependent on the church. This happens in churches of all sizes, but it may be a bigger problem the larger the church. It's worth pondering whether the attractional elements previously mentioned combine with a consumerist mindset to create a passive group of believers who get stuck as 'mere infants' (1 Corinthians 3:1).

Barrier 2: In response to this danger of overdependence on the church, some people question if enough time has been spent intensively and personally growing real disciples. The

charge is that we have too many consumers, and consequently
the church isn't distinctive and thus is not having an impact.
Large churches with big meetings are eyed with suspicion for
caving into cultural pressures or for being over-programmed.[3]
What is needed, it is argued, is less of a 'big meeting' and
more of the intimate disciple-to-disciple relationship. Such
close discipleship relationships can be cultivated avidly.

There is much about this emphasis that is right. I recall a
Christian leader doing something clever with maths at a large
missionary rally. He asked us to imagine that there were
only two real disciples in the whole world, just two. They
worked really hard for a whole year but only managed to make
one disciple each. So now in the whole world there were just
four disciples. They worked really hard, but again they only
managed to make one disciple each in a whole year. At that rate
of growth, how long do you think it would be before the world
was reached for Christ? Just over thirty-seven years! He said that
Jesus, though he spoke to vast crowds, wasn't enamoured by
them and didn't need big numbers to boost his confidence in
the truth, but actually was looking for true disciples. Disciples
who would go and make disciples and not just join a crowd.[4]

Yet I have reservations, for I have sensed that many keen
young pastors see intensive mentoring as the answer to the
lack of maturity and conversion growth. They look at medium-
sized and larger churches and worry that they are stuck in a
rut. Their alternative to 'just running comfortable meetings'
is to pour pastoral and teaching input into a few believers,
hoping they will grow qualitatively and then impact others
for Christ. A lot of intensive pastoral energy becomes focused
on a few.

Such input means that believers should grow, and they may
indeed disciple others. But my experience makes me wary.
Believers will soak up any amount of pastoral care, but it will

not necessarily lead to maturity, service or outreach. Talking to one another, even listening to a good leader, will not necessarily mean that maturity develops. What tends to happen, as pastors deliver ever more intensive input, is that the group laps it all up, becomes dependent on him, and exhibits the group dynamics of an in-house club. An unhealthy 'guru' mindset can develop, where the primary mentor becomes too significant in the growth to Christlike maturity.

Two perils of human nature worth knowing about! Forewarned is forearmed.

Small: growing mature by growing in a small group

So how do you overcome these twin, but opposite, dangers which threaten the growth to maturity?

Remember the maxim: 'If you grow large, you have to grow small at the same time.' Only a few verses into Acts 2, we read that the believers not only met in the temple courts, but they met from house to house too (Acts 2:46). Paul visited from house to house as a pastor in the relatively large church of Ephesus, as well as teaching publicly (Acts 20:20). Maturity develops in the 'both/and' environment of large and small meetings, not the 'either/or'.

Large churches are invariably made up of lots of small groups. Larry Osborne, an American pastor who has led churches of all sizes, authored *Sticky Church*.[5] A key point he makes is that if large attracts, small keeps. Small groups are the place 'where people get velcroed in'. Some kind of organizing around large *and* small is wise.

Many churches today have some such methodology, although quite a few small to medium-sized churches maintain the once ubiquitous 'church Bible study and prayer meeting evening'. Some find it hard to change to another midweek system as they grow. Members fear that dividing will threaten the unity of the church. If the one group divides into two or more, on different nights, it will mean that the pastor will need to be at midweek Bible studies a lot. This will feel like unnecessary duplication. It will also mean that church premises, if owned, are not being used to the full, as the meetings are home-based. So members will wonder what the point is of dividing.

But this is to misunderstand the rationale for small groups. The traditional midweek meeting's main assumption is that knowledge is the missing ingredient. It assumes that more information, given in monologue form, will solve that problem: the saints are being equipped just by listening to more. It doesn't understand that the participatory aspects of small-group meetings compared to one larger midweek meeting are significantly different and more beneficial for discipleship development.

Larger churches experience what the small church doesn't see here, namely that midweek isn't just replicating Sunday, but doing something different to achieve the goal of growing healthy disciples. That's because of the way the numbers dynamics work. The small church's midweek may not feel too different from a Sunday. In a larger church, a home group will feel hugely different from the Sunday gathering.

Some churches will face a problem that tests the mettle of its leaders. As the church grows in numbers, the one midweek meeting almost always fails to grow commensurately. So a threefold growth from, say, thirty to ninety will rarely be reflected in a threefold growth of the midweek from twenty to sixty. What you typically find is that the *proportion* attending the one midweek meeting will go down. You may now have thirty people there, but whereas the midweek once attracted

66% of the church, now it will only be 33% of a church that's grown to ninety.

Re-engineering midweek meetings
Though lack of commitment may well be an issue with some, often the problem is more an organizational one. If you re-engineer the midweek from one night of the week to meetings on several evenings and give people a choice, the attendance will often grow and come to reflect the overall numerical strength of the church once more. When our church changed from one midweek meeting to three home groups, we grew from about 35% to nearly 85% of the church attending, so much so that we had to start new groups very quickly to cope. All that exhorting for more commitment, when all that was really needed was for us to act smarter!

It is better to introduce a structure which gives options at different times, in order to solve the busyness problem. I have seen churches so worried about jeopardizing a sense of unity if they held small groups on different nights that they kept all small groups on the same night, but this didn't deal with the problem they were trying to solve.

Some leaders become very prescriptive about which small group members must attend and allocate people to groups. This can feel very hierarchical. My instinct is to give freedom where freedom can be given. Trust others to make decisions that affect them and don't be over-controlling. Our church gave people freedom to attend the group that suited them best and to decide when to move groups too if their personal circumstances changed. We also handed responsibility over to small-group leaders to recruit new people into their groups.

What we did do was track people by asking leaders to supply the names of those attending their groups. This left us with the names of people who weren't attending a small group, and so this became a list from which leaders of existing and new groups could recruit members. We learned that splitting a growing group was OK the first time, but subsequently members became frustrated that, just as they were beginning to develop relationships, it was all changed. Now we ask for volunteers to start new groups and encourage new people to join them. It isn't always easy for a new person to join a well-established group where everyone seems to know everyone else. A group made up of a sizeable proportion of new people, led by a capable leader, means that all feel they are on the journey together.

Encouraging new people at a Sunday meeting to participate in a small home-group is a key aspect of retaining them. A larger church will need to think carefully about how it scripts the pathway from Sunday to home group, making signposts clear and the journey easy. Otherwise, as we've seen, people will get lost. We have a saying: 'If new people don't connect to the small as well as the large, it is only a matter of time before they leave the large.' The combination of belonging to both has proven to be a great setting in which to foster healthy discipleship.

Time, space and small groups

Some churches organize primarily around the geography of where members live. That may work, but at the start I would not recommend it. Time is the commodity in short supply, and space works at a different scale for different people. What may seem local to one person may appear a long way off for another. Convenience of getting to a small group is more about time management than spatial proximity.

Of course spatial proximity does bring positive benefits. Relationships are more likely if members of a small group live, shop and play in a small area. Yet given people's geographical networks, this isn't a simplistic thing, and small groups don't need to operate on a nearest-neighbour basis to be very effective. It all depends on what you want them to achieve. If it's there that you must make your main friends, spend leisure time together, do community service and evangelism, then proximity is crucial. Yet you may then be expecting small groups to achieve more than they can do well.[6]

What small does for discipleship, large can't do very well at all
Remember that the aim of a small group is not to replicate Sunday, but to do something different. Why is that important? Because, as a church meeting grows larger on a Sunday, some key aspects of Christian development are harder to facilitate. For example, it becomes difficult for many people to take part in audible prayer. Sharing can be done in a large meeting, but the methods of doing this (often through notice sheets or information cards) can become impersonal. There are often limitations in the audio environment, meaning it can be difficult to hear people who are not using microphones. There is also the problem that the greater the numbers, the lower the proportion of people taking part with individual contribution. So some elements of the New Testament emphasis on 'one-anothering' can't easily be achieved through one large meeting (there are fifty-nine references to matters such as 'love one another', 'greet one another' and 'speak to one another').

Our church has worked at dialoguing in various size groups. Sometimes, the teacher asks the questions of the hearers. This is based on the assumption that it's only as a hearer formulates an answer in his or her own words that a teacher can be sure the lesson is truly learned. Jesus used this method with his questions in Matthew 16:13–20. Once he knew they knew, as evidenced in Peter's confession, he moved on to another lesson – which they found hard to stomach (verses 21–28)!

124 READY, STEADY, GROW!

Catechizing (the word translated 'instruction' in Galatians 6:6) is a valuable teaching method. This, however, becomes difficult as numbers grow. Being asked questions as a teacher is another teaching tool. Questions directed to the teacher of a larger group may be possible, but of course the proportion of people who can ask questions in a reasonable time frame declines too. Conversely small groups can excel here.

What to do in small groups

I am slightly wary of the church that organizes its small groups primarily around lengthy Bible studies. The model tends to self-select – the cerebral love it; the rest are not sure it's for them.

There is also the problem of providing really good leaders. Opinionated people discussing a difficult passage of the Bible can tax even the most experienced leader. (In fact, it doesn't have to be a difficult passage, for the people on their own may be problematic enough!) I am not sure that most churches have enough leaders for the detailed studies some select for the home-group system, nor can they train up enough to keep starting new groups as a church grows.

We ended up with a method that Osborne recommends: taking the teaching of the Sunday meeting and developing it further. The teaching pastors have done a lot of the hard work, and then the small groups build on this. This enables us to:

- go more deeply into the Bible;
- apply it more thoroughly into our personal lives; and
- respond more worshipfully than we can do in the large meeting.

In this way, the benefits of growing disciples to maturity flowing from *both* types of settings (clear teaching, joyful worship, encouragement and excitement from the large; personal ownership, honest accountability and meaningful prayer from the small) are not disconnected.

The small also becomes the key place where relational glue develops. Experiencing life with other disciples becomes part of developing a Christian character.

Specialist help: giving focused encouragement

The final part of an organizational strategy to foster healthy discipleship and growth to maturity is to give specialist help. This involves the following.

Investing in leadership training, especially for small-group leaders

The raw material is *people-shaped*. Barnabas-type characters make ideal small-group leaders. Wise, gracious and encouraging are the watchwords. Training them to nurture their groups is a critical part of church and discipleship growth. Their relational skills make people aware that they are connected to something bigger, something that's not impersonal and machine-like.

In a growing church, the pastor needs to commit to this kind of training. As life gets busier, how much busier are you going to get? A wise person said, 'I'd rather train ten people than do the work of ten people.' Investing time and expertise in other people will enable the church to grow beyond your own capacity.

Offering further specialist training for various groups

These could be groups such as marriage preparation, parenting classes, new members' days, youth discussion or an advanced doctrine group. All have their place. Doing separate teaching for alternative groups during the main teaching of the church may be unwise, although perhaps useful now and then. Taking teenagers or even younger children out during the sermon is not a good idea either.

It is crucial that the specialist group doesn't become the place of primary loyalty. Remember that people need to find security, recognition and acceptance. We all too easily form our identity in the group we belong to. The great thing about whole church is that I recognize fellow *believers* as such, and no other determining factor limits fellowship. A specialist forum can all too easily exalt another aspect as the identity marker around which we gather. So beware. Too many churches have found huge problems in getting the Christians in their youth group or even those in their twenties and thirties to identify with the whole church.

To help overcome this, encourage every Christian to attend a small group that is not 'specialism'-based. At a small group, *everyone* mixes with other believers, not necessarily people like themselves.

Fostering one-to-one Bible studies and discussion for those identified as needing extra help

Not-yet-believers feeling their way forward, individuals struggling to overcome an addiction, young Christians hungering for more input, or young women being taught by older women how to live a discipled life (Titus 2:4) may benefit from this. Pair up suitable people and monitor how they go.

One leader told me that the single most pastorally effective thing he ever did was to meet individually and regularly with other men to get them talking about discipleship, until it became a normal part of their life and they felt more confident to lead their own families.

The biggest challenge in giving specialist help is time. To demand too much and create too many options and programmes can make church feel as if it is all about meetings. Remember it's all about people growing more like Jesus.

Large meetings, small groups and specialist environments are places in which Christian maturity can develop. But it's not automatic and doesn't just happen by throwing people together, for 'Unless the LORD builds the house, its builders labour in vain' (Psalm 127:1). If we see Christ build his church through his gospel, the growth to maturity can develop more effectively if the variety of forums the Scriptures describe are intentionally and wisely employed.

Has this chapter uncovered anything in your church that needs addressing or could be done better? Will you be determined that you and the leadership team you belong to will ensure that disciples aren't stunted in their growth? Will you pray that the Holy Spirit will use your actions to cause 'Christ [to be] formed' in those you serve (Galatians 4:19)? Without that happening we will be like self-absorbed infants and not exhibit Christ's loveliness to our communities.

Discussion questions

1. If you were a visitor to your church's largest meeting,
   what do you think you would notice? What would
   stand out, good or bad?
2. Think of other churches you have visited. What could
   churches of each of the size categories do to make their
   main meeting more conducive to discipleship growth?
3. Do your midweek meetings just happen as they always
   have, or is there a development plan to enable them to
   achieve more? How do the participants feel about
   them? What about those who choose not to go?
4. What have you tried and failed in, and tried and
   succeeded in, both in main meetings and small groups?
   What works best in each setting?
5. How well are each of the 'forums' highlighted in this
   chapter preparing you to be like Christ and live for Christ
   in your everyday life? Why might that be or not be?

7. SERVE IN MINISTRY: GETTING TEAMS MOBILIZED

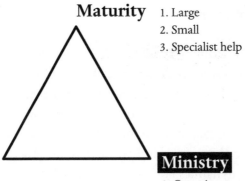

Maturity
1. Large
2. Small
3. Specialist help

Ministry
1. Organize teams
2. Train team leaders
3. Use CARE and SHAPE

Figure 7.1: Ministry map: focus on Ministry

A friend remarked that church is like the *Titanic*. Some do the minimum they're told; they are the cabin boys. Third-class passengers in steerage enjoy the voyage and are not too demanding, but can be pretty passive during crises. Those in

first class love to make demands and give orders, and think
that everyone else is there to serve them. The crew should
have a mentality which says, 'We're here to serve you', but
some can't wait to get off the boat!

As you look at the 'embarkation list' of your church at the
moment, how do the proportions of those types play out?
Lots of passengers, too few workers?

Everyone who follows Jesus, the Servant King, should want
to serve as he did. But if you did a volunteer ratio survey, what
would it look like? Is there a high proportion of members
serving other members in some way, or are a few trying to
keep the whole ship afloat? The leadership challenge is to
ensure that all are actively engaged in serving fellow believers.

So how can a leader effectively facilitate ministry?

The danger of the plateau

A warm and welcoming small church may well grow into a
warm and welcoming medium-sized church. Good teaching,
caring people, shared lives and humble prayerfulness will
likely as not lead to even further growth. But we found in
previous chapters that at this point, when everyone is feeling
very encouraged by growth and saying to themselves, 'We are
enjoying this', dynamics are going to kick in which speak of
tunnels of chaos ahead.

This has also been called the plateau effect. It's the place
where success and comfort combine to prevent the church
taking risks and making changes to keep reaching out with
the gospel. As a leader it's hard to cope with too, for just as
you have overcome so much and everyone is happy, you
realize that staying there will lead to problems. You have to
take action, prompted by your concern to keep getting the

gospel out, but you will also have to be informed by organizational nous.[1]

Wisdom that prevents plateauing

It is precisely at this point that your understanding of church numbers comes in (see chapter 1). Somewhere at the top end of medium-sized, unless a church thinks carefully about how it facilitates service ministry, it will likely fail to grow much larger. Worse, it may begin to decline and go backwards.

The church needs to learn the organization lessons of Acts 6. That wasn't written so that we could say, 'Oh, look how the church overcame the problem of Hebraic and Greek-speaking widows complaining about food – how interesting!' No, it was written so that when we face similar organizational growth problems, we will employ wisdom to overcome them.

Organize teams

As numbers grow, wisdom dictates that you have to rethink and re-engineer how people serve. From a world of a few volunteers, the church needs to move into a culture where all are encouraged to serve somewhere, but no-one is allowed to do too much. The church needs to develop an Acts 6 team structure for all that it does. To engage more of its members as servants, not spectators, we must see that much of the work described in the New Testament was done by small teams.

The Lord Jesus thoroughly prepared a small team, pouring his grace, wisdom and energy into training them and then filling them with his Spirit so that they could accomplish his goals for them. Paul always seemed to work in small teams (see Acts 20:4–5). The times he mentions being on his own bear testimony to the fact he was always working with others (see for example 2 Timothy 4:9). Churches had teams of elders and deacons (Philippians 1:1).

As we know, one of the difficult transition moments is moving a medium / awkward-sized church, accustomed to a few doing a lot, into a fully developed team system where a lot do a little. How can this be achieved?

Acknowledge the problems

Initially, it's no bad thing to describe and discuss some of the symptoms of Acts 6 and what they look like in your church. It is helpful if this problem can be acknowledged for what it is, not a symptom of sinfulness, but an organizational blockage arising out of developing complexity. Give people permission to recognize that things don't always feel good when you grow. Acknowledge the struggles and victories of the past, and emphasize that these could be precursors of good things to come. Talk about members doing fewer things better, rather than getting tired because they are doing more things worse.[2] Once the problem of growth is owned, the leadership can discuss ways forward using a team template.

Map out the tasks

List your tasks and ministries, and think about them as being run by teams, not just a few hard-working volunteers. Organize as much as you can around small groups of people charged to carry out ministry tasks. This will involve Sunday meeting organization, but also community ministry and member-to-member ministry that might otherwise be out of the spotlight, such as visiting the ill or bereaved.

Describe the value of TEAM (Together Everyone Achieves More)
Encourage members to think about where they could serve. You want everyone to serve somewhere. Emphasize that they don't need to be good at everything to serve in a team. For example, someone may not be great at running children's games but could serve up the drinks halfway through, thereby playing a vital part in that team's outreach ministry. Many feel they have to be super-competent to serve, and so we need to stress that in teams all have a valuable role, whatever their capabilities. Together Everyone Achieves More. Teams allow strengths to cover weaknesses.

Give lots of choice and reassurance that people have permission to move on if circumstances change. These are not jobs for life, and indeed one of the big problems of people serving in small churches is that they tend to view their ministry as their personal domain.

Emphasize that less is more
Underscoring a team approach helps everyone do a better job, even if it is in a more restricted area, for they now have ample time to improve what they are doing. They don't have to worry about all the other ministries, but can be thankful that God has gifted others to serve in those areas.

Get ready to go!
Plan for 'new-start' meetings for embryonic teams. As a leader, make sure you are there to give vision and encouragement. Let them dream a bit. Help them to see how each team's work affects the gospel success of the whole church, and emphasize how everyone's input is valued in team-level decision-making.

Once the teams begin to form and perform, older-established members will feel a burden is lifted off their backs in that they don't now have to do everything, and newer people can see ways in which to get involved somewhere.

Train team leaders

Selecting and training leaders is a key aspect of any transition. Growing organizations need capable leaders at every level of church life (remember Exodus 18; leaders of tens, fifties and so on). Character is essential, but then capability is also important to ministry team success. Notice how deacons in 1 Timothy 3:10 are 'tested' first. This could refer to jobs which they carried out to ensure they were able as well as willing. Some leaders are good at certain types of tasks, and not others. There's no shame in that, but it's worth exploring before an inappropriate task is assigned.

The New Testament qualifications for leadership aren't those of superheroes, but reflect a concern for mature Christian character, something within the reach of most believers. Ministry team leaders need to be good with the people who work under them. They also must know how to work with other leaders.[3] Time spent investing in ministry team leaders will pay dividends in church life.

Here are some important things we have found as a church:

Firstly, use empowerment rather than delegation language. The former is heard as: 'I believe in you; this task is important, and I am sure that with some help you can do it.' The latter tends to be heard as: 'I have more important things to do than this job. I am not sure you can do it well, and if you don't come up to scratch, I will complain.'

When we talked about this to our deacons, they saw that a change in vocabulary might really help – and it has done so. Empowerment makes me think more about how I can ensure that the person is supported in accomplishing the task. The leader's responsibility is to ensure the success of their followers. Jack Welch, former CEO of General Electric, said, 'Before you are a leader, success is all about growing yourself. When you become a leader, success is all about growing others.'[4] Empowerment language, in my opinion, makes this more of an intentional goal than just 'delegation'.

Secondly, encourage people not to worry about all the teams they are *not* in. No-one can be part of everything, but members of smaller churches may feel they ought to be. We need, like the apostles, to be happy to '[hand] this responsibility over' (Acts 6:4), so that we can get on with something else that needs doing.

Thirdly, help your teams function. They don't just 'storm, norm, perform and platform' all on their own.[5] Putting names on a rota is not the same as a team working well. I have found Walter Wright's CARE plan invaluable, and developed it to use in our church.[6]

Use CARE and SHAPE

The CARE plan
C = Clarify the mission
See how our team relates to the overall mission of the gospel and the church's work. The janitor who cleaned NASA's toilets reportedly told President Kennedy, 'My job is to help put a man on the moon.'[7] Without this bigger vision, the team is drawn into the humdrum and the mediocre.

A = Agree on specific goals
How do we do the task set before us? How do you deliver 'the best sound possible, given the audio environment of the

original recording'? Let the team figure it out. That's true for
any amount of teamwork. How do you welcome new people
effectively? How will you serve up fresh coffee to 600 people,
so they don't have to queue for half an hour? How will you
learn new songs to enhance worship? How will you ensure
the bereaved are given adequate support once the funeral is
over? The team structure is the way larger churches ensure
things get done.

Using the SMART acronym will help too:

- **S**pecific. What *exactly* is going to be done?
- **M**easurable. Some kind of way to measure things is
  helpful – 'it's going to cost £xx' is often one of them!
  Best to know earlier than later.
- **A**ttainable. Realistic goals that can be accomplished
  given the volunteer or staff resources allocated to the
  task, and in consideration of the overall work of the
  church. These are to be agreed on by the whole
  team and include what is going to be performed
  by whom.
- **R**elevant. Not getting lost in the detail, but doing
  tasks that will make a difference to the team
  performance and to the overall mission. Otherwise,
  focus and alignment are lost, and the church drifts
  off-mission.
- **T**imed. When will the job be done? This key metric
  becomes increasingly important as churches grow,
  because so many people are affected. It shocked me
  when a leader asked why, with 200 people sitting in
  an auditorium, we kept starting five minutes late. Not
  only did this put the preacher under time pressure later
  in the meeting, but it wasted 1,000 *aggregate minutes* of
  others' lives every Sunday morning.

R = *Review your progress*
Christians are often weak here. Any criticism is seen as a
personal affront, and we are not used to learning how to do
better. In teams, we can review what we did and think of ways
to do it better.

We often employ the *Match of the Day 2* (*MOTD2*) method
of '2 good, 2 bad': two things that worked well to thank God
for and two things to improve.[8] As most of us were nervous
about giving and receiving feedback, we started with . . . my
talks. We met monthly to review a service and talked about
what went well in the sermon and how it could have been
more helpful. When everyone saw that I was mortified – no,
I mean encouraged – and that I improved, we started working
on others' roles too. Timothy Keller's paper on being a
'missional church' helped us no end, because it gave us goals
and values to aspire to in conducting our meetings. I would
strongly commend it to you.[9]

All teams will benefit from having an honest look at what
they do and then improving. People love to serve in teams
that do things excellently. Few like being in a team that has
settled for the ordinary. We want to serve in something that
is valued by others and is a blessing to them. Remember
Paul's words to slaves: 'Whatever you do, work at it with
all your heart, as working for the Lord, not for men, since
you know that you will receive an inheritance from the
Lord as a reward. It is the Lord Christ you are serving'
(Colossians 3:23, 24). Serving with excellence is something
to aspire to.

E = *Equip your people*
Commit to training individuals and the team. This may mean
a course: food handling for those in catering, administration
for those in a church office, or a piece of kit taking a team's

capability forward. There are endless ways of helping teams to do a better job.

Use this CARE template at team meetings. It really helps to focus discussion and give direction. Walter Wright has provided the church with a wise processing tool that is not to be neglected!

SHAPE

Of the various ways to help people understand how they can serve God, Rick Warren's SHAPE acronym is a helpful starter:[10]

- **S**piritual gifts
- **H**eart (passions and interests)
- **A**bilities
- **P**ersonality factors (such as introversion or extraversion)
- **E**xperiences God has used to mould us so that we can be a blessing to others.

Earlier I mentioned the induction/new members' day. As well as allowing people to discuss a little about individuals' identities and the background to the church, it also covers how they became Christian believers and what we as a church believe, their commitments and our church values, and finally how they can serve in a team and what 'SHAPE' they are.[11] During the induction day, we encourage people to consider where they can serve and get them to sign up for a team. As mentioned earlier, we also make team leaders aware of new people. This intentionality significantly helps new people to start serving more effectively.

Resourcing

As your church gets larger, you will need staff support, finance and proper eldership oversight. A larger church may need some kind of manager of ministry teams (sometimes called an executive pastor in the USA) who translates leadership and membership aspirations into real and positive changes on the ground. Ministries need careful supervision to ensure that high ethical standards are upheld, and good-quality aesthetics are maintained. If either go downhill, both the church's and the gospel's reputations will be threatened.

It is reckoned that for every two frontline church workers (such as pastor-teacher, evangelist, community worker), it takes one support worker to help take things forward properly.[12] A church will need to plan and budget accordingly. Without this plan in place, a church's growth may stall, not because of a failing in its gospel presentations, but because of administrative blockages. Or without the resourcing of ministry teams, the church could just become a preaching centre and not develop its community impact.

Results

But can changing to a team structure actually work and make a difference? We started small, but re-engineered at a critical time. It took many discussions and much planning and effort. Once the team structure was in place, new people started serving, and long-established members got their life back. This opened a door for further Word ministry, as well as Deed ministry, as our preachers could concentrate on areas for which they were gifted and entrust important measures to others. As the church had developed this essential team structure before we had 200 attending, it hasn't had to change as we have transitioned from awkward-sized into large.[13]

Two significant results flow from service ministry:

1. It is a powerful witness to anyone being served. It speaks loudly of *the Servant* and his ministry of grace to the undeserving. It often disarms criticisms and softens hearts to the gospel.
2. Serving alongside brothers and sisters helps to mature believers. It develops character in ways that mere discussion can't.

The large church doesn't mean busier individuals. Indeed, by serving in a limited number of teams, members have more time to develop relationships with those far from God than is sometimes the case in smaller churches.

Don't try to do too much; large doesn't have to mean omni-competent. But make sure ministries are resourced well. We want those we serve in the community to know we are there for the long term.

It is crucial that leaders acknowledge the work that team members do. This is especially true for those who serve in unseen ways that ordinarily wouldn't get much recognition. Acknowledging service to God is a key part of encouraging and motivating them. Notice how Paul thanks God for works of service, but tells people that he has done so in so many of his letters. (See for example Romans 1:8–9; 1 Corinthians 1:4–5; Ephesians 1:16–17.) Acknowledgment and appreciation go much further than many leaders realize. It is not flattery to tell people we are grateful to God for their service.

Service will mean getting up when others don't, putting a towel on your arm, bending your knees and getting your hands dirty – with your eyes on the Master who served you. His recognition and appreciation – 'Well done, good and faithful servant' – will truly be more than enough reward (Matthew 25:21, 23).

Discussion questions

1. What's good about a teamwork approach in accomplishing tasks and achieving goals? Conversely, what makes teams toxic or underachieving? What have you learned in this chapter that can help keep teams healthy and functioning effectively?

2. Is it time to rethink some of your church's ministries? Do some feel very tired? Have people been doing the same old things with the same old results for too long? Could you get volunteers or team members together to pray for the Spirit to breathe new life into them?

3. Is it time you invested in more intentional team-leader training? Could you read some leadership material outside of your normal range? Could you be bold enough to close some ministries down, at least for a while, to create a bit of space in an overly busy church?

4. If you are in a small church, how could the CARE plan still help you as a whole group – the team that the church in effect is at the moment?

5. If you are in a medium-sized church, perhaps get some feedback from people who have to obey those in leadership. How does it feel to have to carry out delegated tasks? How could you (or others) improve their experience?

6. If you find yourself in a growing awkward-sized church, how can you encourage the 're-engineering' of tasks, so that teams begin to function well? If you are in a team, does it feel like you serve together on a productive team or is it more like just a name on a rota? Which parts of the CARE plan are working best, and which are not working at all?

7. If you are part of the leadership of large church, what are your plans for: (a) introducing new people into the serving activity of the church; and (b) training team leaders to lead their teams effectively? If you were a newcomer, what would worry you about serving in such a large group?

8. Could you inspire people with the grander vision of what ministry is all about? Does heaven's love touching earth's need grab your heart yet? Pray until it does. Then let others feel your passion for serving.

8. REACH OUT IN MISSION: 'COME AND SEE' CREATES WINS FOR EVERYONE

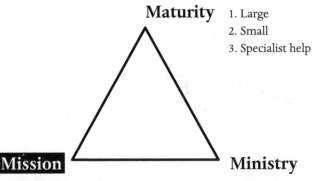

Maturity 1. Large
2. Small
3. Specialist help

Mission
1. *Provide Come and See*
2. Promote Care and Serve
3. Prepare for Go and Tell

Ministry
1. Organize teams
2. Train team leaders
3. Use CARE and SHAPE

Figure 8.1: Ministry map: focus on Mission: Come and See

'Gospel' means 'good news'. It's a *message* proclaiming that God is reconciled to his worst enemies by the blame-taking death of his Son and all who believe his message begin a new life. Christians have received and believed this good news, and one would expect that they would naturally tell others. Some do. Many struggle. And most feel failures.

Churches often fare no better. Many leaders are worried that much growth feels like attracting and recycling Christians, with a sprinkling of converts added now and then. Few think they are seeing significant inroads. As many as 97% of the UK population, over 60 million people, do not claim a personal saving relationship with God through the Lord Jesus Christ.

Of the three areas God wants us to be committed to, this one presents the greatest challenges. Here is where churches of all sizes need the most help. So at the end of each of the next three chapters, I am going to offer some 'growth suggestions', tailored to different-sized churches. Look out for yours, but read the others too – there may be things you can adapt for your church.

Happily, we aren't left to our own devices. The Lord speaks in his Word and speaks clearly. For Acts 16 represents a description of how the gospel can reach every city, town, village and hamlet.[1] If you care about gospel progress, this passage merits your very careful attention. I suggest that you read it again before going further.

The gospel journey

'One small step for a missionary, one giant leap for Christianity' comes to mind, as in Acts 16 the gospel comes to Europe for the first time. Paul is supernaturally kept from places in Asia Minor. Note Luke's favourite threefold emphasis when he wants to underline something: 'having been kept by the Holy Spirit from preaching the word in . . . Asia . . . they tried to enter Bithynia, but the Spirit of Jesus would not allow them to' (Acts 16:6–7), and then the positive call: 'During the night Paul had a vision of a man of Macedonia standing and begging him, "Come over to Macedonia and help us."' Luke signals that they got the message, for 'After Paul had seen the vision, we got ready at once to leave for Macedonia, concluding that God had called us to preach the gospel to them' (Acts 16:10). This was a continent where ignorance, godlessness, barbarity and immorality mingled with advanced civilization. Just as spiritually tough as now, it was filled with the sceptical and the superstitious, those with a blind faith in other gods who were no gods at all, a range of phenomenal vices and all the corruption huge amounts of money and power can bring. It was populated by those who were 'dead in trespasses and sins' (Ephesians 2:1 KJV). No wonder it needed such a direct intervention by God; who would choose to come here?

Gospel success
Luke chooses three stories to illustrate the power of the gospel. They may seem unconnected until you recall the regularly recited Jewish male prayer:

> Blessed are you, Hashem, King of the Universe, that you did not make me a Gentile. Blessed are you, Hashem, King of the Universe, that you did not make me a slave. Blessed are you, Hashem, King of the Universe, that you did not make me a woman.

The duty promoted by religion doesn't have much to say to help. But the good news of what the living God has done in his Son can break through all barriers and bring new life.

Luke shows the gospel reaching very dissimilar people – a woman, a slave and a Gentile – and in different ways. Whereas the message is prominent in all three, *how* the person comes into contact with it varies. I am going to use each story to help churches develop strategies for reaching people, devoting a chapter to each one.

A woman reached by Word ministry

Let's look at the woman, Lydia, first. We are told two significant things: she is rich and she is religious. She is rich from
the luxury goods import/export trade. Purple cloth was a
favourite for citizens who retired to colonies (little Romes)
like Philippi. The dye was rare and expensive and had to be
brought in from abroad. The woman runs a household and
can invite a group of people back to her large home for lunch
immediately (the place where the brothers all meet at the end
of the story; see Acts 16:40). She is religious, a 'God-fearer',
and attends a place of worship to carry out a classic religious
duty, prayer, even before the gospel is explained to her.

In that meeting setting, Lydia is reached by Word ministry.
It's not Paul's brilliance, clarity or charisma which the Bible
emphasizes. No, *God* 'opened her heart to respond' to the
gospel (verse 14). Even when we have carefully prepared and
helpfully delivered the message, it is never about our ability to
save someone. As Paul said to the Corinthians, he and Apollos
were 'only servants' through whom they heard the Word, and
'only God' could give the increase (1 Corinthians 3:5–7).

There are many religious people around today. This story
teaches that the religious need the gospel of Christ as much
as anyone. Why? It's only when the beauty of Christ's gracious
sacrifice for them captivates their heart that they respond to
God's will with a desire to see him glorified. Deep peace
replaces either the self-righteousness or the deep personal
sense of guilt and failure that religious duty inculcates. Duty
carried out even 'for the one true God' doesn't have the power
to replace our locked-in selfishness and ingrained desire to
serve God *for what we get from him*. In Christ we get *him* and
find he fulfils the deepest desires of our heart. Love, joy
and peace are the result flowing out from within us (Galatians
5:22–23). Millions of religious people need the freedom that

only the gospel brings. Giving them the opportunity to hear the message is crucial.

A new life begins

We see Lydia and her household's response. It seems that just another religious deed is being carried out when they are baptized. Yet this is the signal of a new life: 'Those who belong to Christ Jesus have crucified the sinful nature with its passions and desires' (Galatians 5:24); 'We were therefore buried with him through baptism into death in order that, just as Christ was raised from the dead through the glory of the Father, we too may live a new life' (Romans 6:4). The outward sign speaks of a changed inner reality. Believing the message has brought Lydia into a new relationship with God. Now she is 'a new creation', indwelt by the Spirit of God, under the power of a new affection.

Immediately, Lydia signals her change of direction. She uses her wealth to be a blessing to others: 'If you consider me a believer in the Lord . . . come and stay at my house' (Acts 16:15). She persists in this until 'she persuaded us' (Acts 16:15b). Her resources are placed at the disposal of the gospel, just as our own should be once we have 'tasted that the Lord is good' (1 Peter 2:2).

The importance of an invite

There are many opportunities for Word ministry to reach people today. For there will be people who, if invited, will come along to a meeting where they hear a message from God's Word.

We should take a leaf out of Andrew and Philip's book for, whenever they are mentioned, they connect people to Jesus:

Andrew, Simon Peter's brother, was one of the two who heard
what John had said and who had followed Jesus. The first thing
Andrew did was to find his brother Simon and tell him, 'We
have found the Messiah' (that is, the Christ). And he brought
him to Jesus.
(John 1:40–42)

At another encounter:

Finding Philip, [Jesus] said to him, 'Follow me.' Philip, like
Andrew and Peter, was from the town of Bethsaida. Philip found
Nathanael and told him, 'We have found the one Moses wrote
about in the Law, and about whom the prophets also wrote – Jesus
of Nazareth, the son of Joseph.' 'Nazareth! Can anything good
come from there?' Nathanael asked. 'Come and see,' said Philip.
(John 1:43–46)

Later we read:

Now there were some Greeks among those who went up to
worship at the Feast. They came to Philip, who was from
Bethsaida in Galilee, with a request. 'Sir,' they said, 'we would
like to see Jesus.' Philip went to tell Andrew; Andrew and Philip
in turn told Jesus.
(John 12:20–22)

The first words from the woman at the well who had just
found eternal life herself, as she told others in her town, were,
'Come, see a man . . . the Christ' (John 4:29). They did, and
that led them to believe for themselves: 'We no longer believe
just because of what you said; now we have heard for
ourselves, and we know that this man really is the Saviour of
the world' (John 4:42).

Then there is Matthew's first act on becoming a follower of Jesus:

> 'Follow me,' Jesus said to him, and Levi got up, left everything and
> followed him. Then Levi held a great banquet at his house, and a
> large crowd of tax collectors and others were eating with them.
> But the Pharisees and the teachers of the law who belonged to
> their sect complained to his disciples, 'Why do you eat and drink
> with tax collectors and "sinners"?' Jesus answered them, 'It is not
> the healthy who need a doctor, but the sick. I have not come to
> call the righteous, but sinners to repentance.'
> (Luke 5:27–32)

No wonder the American church leader, Bill Hybels, calls events where you find a whole load of people far from God together with a few followers of Christ 'Matthew parties'.[2]

'Come and See'

Andrew and Philip's habit, along with these other examples, emphasizes one of the strategies that leaders can use to encourage mission: the 'Come and See' strategy. It builds on invitations to hear a message, as Lydia did that wonderful day.

Dave Bennett did a master's research thesis into Christian conversion in the UK.[3] He undertook in-depth questionnaires of nearly 400 adult converts who became believers between 1995 and 2002. As each person told their story, much as Luke tells us Lydia's, they were asked to describe what was significant in their conversion.

He found that there was a link to an early exposure to Christianity, with 88% of females and 84% of males saying they had had some contact with a church during childhood.

That's a great encouragement to parents and to those who work with children and young people.

Another factor was the importance of relationships: 92% had had a relationship with a Christian before they were converted and 86% said it was significant in their conversion. Most adults coming to faith are helped by a friendship with a Christian they know and trust, and 87% said they knew of someone praying for them before they became a Christian. Recently we had a lady who was converted; her son had been praying for her for over thirty years since his own conversion.

What really excited me were Bennett's findings about invitations. Of the converts he interviewed, 87% were given some kind of invitation to an event: 'This is one of the key findings of this study – that, second only to praying for them, giving an invitation was the most significant way Christians had helped.'[4] He tells of one lady who was invited to carol services by a friend for fifteen years before she said 'yes' and attended. This became a key step on her pathway to Christ.

When a 'no' is a gospel win

This revolutionized my thinking. I knew that many Christians didn't invite people to events, because they thought, 'They will say "no", so what's the point even of asking them?' Bennett found that even when people said 'no', they appreciated being asked and it was still a positive thing compared to not being asked at all.

Did you get that? Even when people said 'no', it was a positive gospel win and not the utterly negative rejection that Christians assume it is.

Many have not cultivated friendships or think they can only invite people when they have developed very deep friendships indeed over years. Ironically, it doesn't need to be like that. We should call it 'acquaintanceship' rather than 'friendship' evangelism. It's the circle of people I know and who know me, but we don't have to be 'best pals' before they receive an invite.

So I realized the problem . . . is in the heads of Christian believers! Armed with that knowledge, I redoubled my efforts at encouraging Christians to invite people to settings like Lydia's where they could hear something of the faith.

The journey to faith

Lydia was converted the first time she heard – wouldn't we all want converts like that? Most, however, are on a longer journey. People may come to an event, and it may seem as if nothing is accomplished. Yet just meeting some Christians with whom they have some fun or a nice conversation can take away suspicion and move them towards faith.

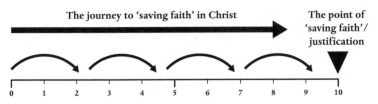

Figure 8.2: The journey to 'saving faith' in Christ

If we think of Lydia as coming *to*, and crossing the line *at the point* of saving faith on that Saturday morning (beginning a new journey *of* faith) and call that '10' on a scale 0–10, we have to realize that many people and life events had been used by God to move her along from her original '0' to that point. In that journey, 0–1 is huge too. Compared to the '10' of coming to salvation, it doesn't seem so. Yet it still counts. (It's like golf – all strokes count as a score, be it a 3-inch putt or a 300-yard drive.) If a church wants to see people moving from 9 to 10, it also needs to invest time and energy to help people move from 0 to 1, 4 to 6 or 7 to 9.

Richard Meryon, former leader of Christian Vision for Men, told of his time as Chief Engineer on an aircraft carrier, HMS *Ark Royal*. Landing an aircraft on a heaving deck is quite a skill. The process starts when planes are tracked on radar from over the horizon. The sailors may see only the last few hundred yards, but it is a long process. Similarly, he argued, when we attempt to reach men today, we need to understand that many will first need friendship builders where they have some fun, eat some food and grow in confidence, rubbing shoulders with Christians. He stressed that even before this is organized, individual Christians will need to be making relationships of trust and likeability with people they know. If there's no contact with colleagues, mates, neighbours and relatives, there will be nobody to invite.[5]

Then come events with 'gospel tasters', something worth listening to, causing unbelievers to think. After that, for those who want more, there can be a course, an offer of a one-to-one reading of the Bible or an invite to church.

Some events may be used by God to move people along the early part of that 0–10 scale. We shouldn't despise these. In some, the Word will be more implicit: a church picnic in the park causing people to say, 'These people are really friendly and very welcoming.' Others will be explicit, for example, seven weeks of Christianity Explored, which is very Word-intensive.

Norman Stone, the Christian TV producer, gave a helpful communication rule of thumb: 'You can say a little to a lot, or a lot to a little, but rarely a lot to a lot.'[6] This helps us realize just how valuable those early-stage low-key events are, and keeps us from worrying that 'the whole counsel of God' (see Acts 20:27) wasn't communicated at one go.

Creating an invite culture

A leader will need to do three things to create a culture where it is normal to invite people to events:

1. Encourage Christians to see with compassion the people all around them and foster a desire for them to win them for Christ. Armed with Dave Bennett's findings about the importance of relationships in conversions, Christians need reminding to see the people they already know as those most likely to be converted next. They should be expectant of all that God can do through their normal, but prayerful, interaction with people all day long.
2. Create multiple entry points for the gospel: a variety of events for people at different stages of the journey. A balance of these can be held over a period of time. Some events will be friendship builders, others will be gospel tasters and some will be a more prolonged exposure to the truth.
3. Urge Christians actually to invite people to events.

It needs a lot more energy and encouragement for an invite culture to take root than leaders realize. But when does a Boeing 747, loaded with 50,000 gallons of fuel, 600 passengers and all their luggage, and weighing over 900,000 lbs, need maximum thrust? At take-off! So for a church to get away from maintenance mode, it will need energy from leaders to change the habits of decades.

'Happy Christmas . . . I'd love it if . . . '
If organizing 'Come and See' is a good way to foster real growth as a result of the gospel getting to new places, then

it's worth working extra hard to see it develop. And Christmas is a great place to start. We can invite *anyone we know* to a church carol service – with a big smile and a friendly ask. Most people will say, 'No' – it may be competing with *Sports Personality of the Year* on TV. But some will say, 'I'd love to', and you might be surprised that a church of just thirty could hold a carol service with a hundred present – so long as the invites are *personal* and not leaflets through a door. That is key. Remember that people like to be asked, even if they say 'no'. The impersonal doesn't go far with people today in an era of junk mail.

Leaders should model this. Too many pastors, vicars, ministers and elders *challenge* members to bring people, but don't do it themselves. Once *you* start, others will begin to catch the vision that God reaches people through Word settings.

You can go and personally ask neighbours two or three doors either side of you and give them a warm invite to a carol service. You know their faces; they know yours. They may be of no faith or another faith, but a positive invite will go miles.

Ask people from your leisure activities too. And if you are a minister, you will bump into some who are not-yet Christians. Maybe you speak at a school, so you could ask the head or the person who facilitates your speaking there. You could invite those on your Christmas card list living locally – maybe some friends you made when your children were at school. If your children are still at school, you (or your spouse) can ask all the people you smile to at the gate. Once you think about it, you could ask a lot of people to a carol service. Some may come. And what is true for you, using some initiative and imagination, needs communicating to the whole church, for the same will be true for them too. Every member knows people who can be invited at Christmas, and this is still culturally acceptable almost everywhere in the UK, Europe and many countries around the world.

Any size of church can work at this, for it's not just the province of the biggest. Years ago, our medium-sized church had a normal carol service. We put leaflets through doors and waited to see who might show up. We had a few (all right then, a tiny handful) of visitors most years. But then we began to seize the day. We really started to encourage people to invite others. We showed them it was normal to invite anyone they knew. We reminded them, 'Don't say people's "no" for them.' We also underlined that a 'no' was not a problem; it was still a positive contact with someone, rather than no contact at all. We hired a much bigger hall. We called the event the Community Carol Service. We invited the local mayor. He was delighted to be asked and came! We all invited like mad and had over 300 new people turn up – we usually had about a hundred attending altogether. People realized, 'It can be done.'

I need to be honest here and confess. I encouraged all of this, but I wasn't optimistic. Temperamentally, I am more of a pessimist than even the 'glass half-empty' person. Those setting out the hall put out all the chairs: 400. When I saw what they had done, I thought they were being ridiculous. I put about half away. Out they had to come again. 'O you of little faith.' I am not allowed to forget that day – and rightly so!

A serious word of advice: make sure you sing traditional carols that people expect. I heard of some new Christians being disappointed when their church used the Street Bible for a Christmas outreach service. The whole thing bombed and their visiting relatives felt alienated. Being too trendy was a bigger barrier than being traditional, ironically!

Yet we aren't naive about all this. People come because it's the time of the year, rather than because of a direct interest in Christ. In a culture losing its sense of Christian heritage, however, don't underestimate the impact of large numbers coming to Christmas services. Many never go inside a church (building), and to have a positive experience helps break down barriers to further gospel exposure. For young adults in particular, this may be an eye-opening experience, and they may begin to question why their culture so prejudicially misrepresents Christianity. Beyond that, we have seen significant numbers progress in their journey to faith and some have even become believers. It all started by being invited to a carol service.

This is a great way for Christians to discover that inviting people is not difficult. Warm feedback about how friendly it all was, plus seeing the whole church achieve more than any individual could on their own, gives a positive sense of gospel impact. A 'win' here can foster a habit of inviting friends to other things.

Once the church sees it can be done, they will follow your lead. And if you are the minister, this change from being a leader-as-preacher to a leader-as-model / example / equipper is an important mindset shift, both for you and for the church. Instead of just telling people how it should be done, you show it, and then the call to 'follow me' is so much more powerful (1 Corinthians 11:1; also recall comments about Paul and Timothy in Philippians 2:18–19).

In churches of varying sizes, this will work slightly differently. In small or medium-sized churches, the leader will model to the whole church what inviting, for example, looks like. In larger churches, the leader will model to other leaders, who in turn model to their smaller groups of followers (for example, their home group) what the desired practice is. A leader of a larger church can't be immediately accessible to all, nor can he possibly cope with all the pastoral demands of everyone, but by investing in modelling, he can release others into effective work, and not become a theoretician aloof from reality.

This needs some structuring and intentional time allocation. Otherwise the urgent wins over the important, and the diary becomes crowded out. So leaders must deliberately plan to invest in those who will become good models to others, spending time with the strongest believers so that they can help the weaker. This seems counter to the idea that the pastor spends all his non-preaching and preparation time with the neediest people and pastoral problems. The latter has to change if the church is to grow and it needs explaining to the church. Members will then realize that though the leader still does pastoral work, he can't now be every individual's pastor, but is training others to share that work with him who will in turn show at accessible, small-group level what good Christian practice looks like.

Creating more invite wins

Like many churches, we have a 'meal with a message' in the form of an autumn supper. These are now so well attended that we hold them on two adjacent nights, giving everyone a chance to bring friends. But we started very small. The problem was not that of organizing the catering or finding a suitable speaker, but getting people there in the first place. Church members kept saying, 'I don't know anybody who would come.' They sensed coming to a supper *with a message* implied a greater degree of interest would be required than at Christmas, and most were reluctant to take that step.

This is a common problem: Christians perceive that friends aren't interested and conclude that it is a waste of time inviting them. To counter this negativity, I gave members beautifully produced invite cards and suggested people I knew they knew, whom they could ask. A small/medium-sized church pastor can do that! Then I regularly asked if they had had responses. We made a great deal of these in prayer meetings and circulated the names so that everyone could pray at home. On the night, we put on the best buffet food possible. People sat with their guests, so that no-one had to meet lots of strangers. You could only come if you brought someone. But everyone else was involved too. Some babysat, many provided food, some decorated the hall, others served food and waited on the tables, while a wonderful team did the washing-up. We debriefed at midweek meetings, with people telling stories about gospel conversations, and we all kept praying. It was a case of: 'Everyone is in this, and some of us happen to have friends who came.' It took a few such events for members to realize that *friends will come*, and, more importantly, God is with us as we bring the gospel to people in culturally appropriate ways. Our part was to act as obedient servants who go, find and bring (see Luke 14:15–24).

I could tell stories of where churches put on meals with a message, but only Christians turned up because no-one had personally invited guests and the ambiance was something like 'Fred's lay-by shack'. Yet I'd rather tell you of others' progress. One small church, with a membership of fewer than twenty, regularly hires a local Indian restaurant and packs it out with eighty or more guests who hear a gospel presentation after their meal. Again, this kind of thing isn't out of the reach of small/medium-sized churches.

Would you like to come to church?
Could your church more positively encourage invites to Sunday services? We were helped by Timothy Keller pointing out that services need to be accessible to outsiders.[7] Far more than an environmental issue (though lighting, sound, coffee,

childcare and other issues are important), it's the mindset of those who speak up front that counts. Speak *as if* the place is full of those present for the first time. The church needs to think about the principle of intelligibility, as in, for example, 1 Corinthians 14:23–25:

> So if the whole church comes together and everyone speaks in tongues, and some who do not understand or some unbelievers come in, will they not say that you are out of your mind? But if an unbeliever or someone who does not understand comes in while everybody is prophesying, he will be convinced by all that he is a sinner and will be judged by all, and the secrets of his heart will be laid bare. So he will fall down and worship God, exclaiming, 'God is really among you!'

So gone are the in-house notices that alienate new people by proclaiming, 'Tuesday A is not at Jill and John's now but is at Pete and Penelope's', which actually communicates to newcomers, 'You don't know what and who I am talking about because you don't belong.' Instead, there's a constant sense of: 'Try to hear how this would sound if you were listening for the first few times yourself.' The way a leader welcomes everyone, and introduces the songs, prayers, Bible readings and other people who take part, can all be done in a way that is much more accessible.[8]

Speaking as someone who came from a non-religious background, I am constantly disappointed at how poorly churches welcome people to their meetings, let alone speak in ways that can be readily understood. I know that Sunday worship is when the church gathers to worship the Lord; it is not to be determined by the cultural mores of the surrounding dominant group. It should, nevertheless, be intelligible at the very least.

The messenger too has to work hard at communicating the unchanging truth of the Bible to the fast-moving world of the audience. Too many preachers assume that non-Christians aren't present, and don't address some of the defeater beliefs (the common assumptions people hold to that make Christianity seem unbelievable) in their minds.[9]

This is important for visitors, but it also sends the message to church members: 'If you bring friends, you can be sure they will be welcomed *as guests*; we will be sensitive to them, and they won't be insulted or alienated by anything other than the message of the cross.' It gives members confidence to invite people directly to church.

That's important because Bennett found that forty-nine people in his sample reported that being invited directly to a church's Sunday service was very significant in their conversion. Many Christians think it is too pushy to invite people directly to church, but really we should be more positive as leaders in facilitating this. Nelson Searcy's book, *Fusion: Turning First-time Guests into Fully Engaged Members of Your Church*, describes the important *first seven minutes* of visiting a church service. He argues that most visitors make up their minds to return or not return in that time-slot. Welcome, signage, facilities, decor, friendliness, clarity of purpose and so on are the issues that affect that decision. You may not agree with all of it, but it will make you think.[10]

Why Men Hate Going to Church by David Murrow will also help you consider ways in which the church's subculture can alienate the average bloke.[11] Murrow comments that navigating church services requires skills that many men don't think they have, or which they perceive women have in greater abundance. Meeting overly familiar greeters at the entrance, having to ask for advice about facilities, not being embarrassed about your children, having to sing in public, mixing with strangers afterwards, making polite conversation, concentrating on talks which may be dull and irrelevant, participating in something cringey such as 'passing the peace'. You get the idea. You may not be able to change everything missionally to accommodate men, but you can think of some ways to help them.

However, we shouldn't be too nervous of inviting people to church, whatever progress we may have made in some of these things. Where God's people love him and love one another, a powerful witness is given, and church on a Sunday can be an excellent place for people to hear God's enduring Word. The psalmist said years ago, 'The unfolding of your words gives light.' It still does.

Multiple entry points

Multiple entry points and clear pathways are important. For some, Sunday services really are a bridge too far. So organize a range of events to which people can be invited. Taking the opportunity to ask someone to something they would enjoy is within the reach of many Christians.

Women in our church run a group called Activate, and the men have one called Yorkie ('It's not for girls'). The rule of thumb is you can come if you bring someone, though that's not watertight, as it is always good for Christians to mix with others' friends anyway. In their planning, they ask the question: 'What would friends most like to come to?' Sometimes members have been surveyed for insights, and programmes developed in response. It is most definitely about being missional with friends.

Invest in excellent publicity. Plan for some events at minimal cost, though a range can be developed to suit all interests and pockets. And don't expect everyone to come to everything. That's a mistake some churches make and it ends up with jaded people. Say, 'Come to what you and your friends find interesting.' Some events will just build friendships and facilitate conversations. Activate has just had a spa therapy day and will soon have a visit to a chilli farm. The blokes had a golf day where a Christian golf pro talked about his life and faith after an *excellent* day out on the course (perhaps reflecting my feelings, as our team scored a three under par, though it was a Texas scramble – the golf-playing reader will understand!). Soon some are off to Normandy for a battlefield tour, and others are going on a water-skiing trial at a newly opened venue. Use wisdom – blokes in particular may need quite a few friendship builders before they are confident enough to hear more.

If people come to an event or two a year, that will be a strong enough platform to invite them to something with more of a taster of the gospel. Small and medium-sized churches may feel at a disadvantage reading this, but here may be an area where cooperation with others is a key. I know of churches that team up with others to help run events. Could your church consider that?

Faith spelt R I S K

Keep reminding Christians to pray and bring people along to something spiritually further down track. If you push people faster than they want to go, you will lose them, but if you don't encourage them to move forward at all, you will lose them too. So we gently prod members to invite people to something with a bit more content to see whether their friends want more. Most Christians are more cautious than they need to be. Many friends are more open than we expect.

We used to wait until we had signs of real interest before we planned Explore[12] or Identity[13] courses. They ended up being few and far between, and numbers weren't large

– perhaps two or three non-Christians brought by a similar number of Christians. A church leader challenged me to book the course in faith and trust God to send the people. That's not my temperamental style, but I rebuked myself, asking, 'Why not give it a go?' We have been doing that for over ten years now and, without fail, we have had people come. Sometimes numbers have been what we had before; mostly though, it's been a very significant increase.

As members have brought friends along, they have realized (the Christians, that is!) that the courses are very welcoming and anybody could find them helpful. So larger numbers of believers have begun to adopt the habit of asking people to courses with significant gospel content.

Don't be discouraged

All this has taken time to develop. Don't be discouraged if you are in a smaller church and it seems tough. In his book, *Good to Great*, Jim Collins discusses an aspect of what makes an organization great and calls it 'the power of the flywheel'. Getting going initially seems so hard; it's like pushing a huge and heavy flywheel on a large machine. But as you put the needed energy in, over time it begins to pick up speed, and the momentum of the flywheel means that things move faster.[14]

We have certainly found that with initiatives to create an invite culture. What once seemed a battle for the mind of believers so they would more positively say 'Come and See' is now an ingrained habit for many. It is bearing fruit, with larger numbers of outsiders coming along to a whole host of events. People are getting converted, by the grace of God, as they hear and believe the gospel.

It's been helpful being a pastor of one church for a long time (I am now in my thirty-first year) and to have seen the church grow through various size categories. It has also been helpful from the point of view of seeing Christians gradually adopt a helpful missional habit, and to see the journeys to faith of many people.

Three key lessons

Firstly, planning Come-and-See events is the easiest way to get the maximum numbers of Christians actively involved in mission outreach to people they know. Even the youngest or most nervous of believers can go and ask. It creates some big wins. It helps believers progress to a much more outward-looking and evangelistically shaped life. In the next couple of chapters, I am going to describe two other aspects of the mission strategy of Acts 16, but I want to underscore that this one is where you start, whatever size you are.

Secondly, results from Come and See will vary. Success is not automatic; this is not a conveyor belt in any sense. Praise God when the journey to faith happens in a morning like Lydia, but usually it is more like ten years! If people know that, then they don't feel quite so defeated if their friends spend time making progress or are not ready for the final steps to faith just yet. Though we know that until they believe the gospel they are in deep peril, we can trust God to work in their hearts as we pray that a series of invite events will be used by the Holy Spirit.

Finally, relationships need to be real and not 'fake smiles'. Sometimes a dichotomy is set up: 'programmes/big church versus relationships/small-missional church'.[15] I have sympathy with that and have seen the negative results of churches losing sight of those far from God, churches preoccupied with manning their ministries and so busy that everyone is worn out. Yet it doesn't have to be that way. This is another case of either/or when it could be both/and. Christians in any size of church, living obedient and gospel-shaped lives, will have lots of relationships.

Growth suggestions for churches of different sizes

Small churches

- Food and friendship are strengths a small church can play to. Summer barbecues, a Christmas bring-and-share party at a member's house and a picnic at a park, wood or beach are events that are cheap and easy to run.
- Large-scale Alpha or Christianity Explored courses will be beyond reach, but an offer of one-to-one Bible reading may be gladly accepted and very effective. Learn to foster these.
- Never let a newcomer leave without asking what they are doing for lunch or supper, and offer them food, even if most invites won't be taken up. Such an extension of friendship goes a very long way.

Medium-sized churches

- If the building is getting full at Christmas events, branch out and hire something bigger – it may be a hotel lounge or a bigger school – anything with space. This will stretch faith for sure, but members may not only rise to the challenge, but be captured by a vision that the church could be a great deal larger. The experience will be a very positive one to nurture future expectation.

- If your leadership doesn't feel they have the skills to run brilliant evangelistic courses, don't be afraid to utilize the excellent DVD-based courses available. Get leaders to attend these so that they grow in confidence and can genuinely recommend them to other members.
- Get leaders/preachers to act as the main greeters on the door on the way in. That way, they will notice new and old alike. The tradition of leaders in the vestry (or the equivalent) before the service may not be the best way of connecting to newcomers, but being at the door as a friendly face probably is.

Awkward-sized churches

- Before new people get too busy in church life, make sure you find out about their circle of acquaintances (family, friends, new neighbours, colleagues). Encourage them to invite them to suitable events, and then make sure you get to know them too. A leader getting alongside new people is a key element in growing medium and awkward-sized churches.
- Schedule regular courses for those who say, 'I'm (a bit) interested.' Don't wait until you have a crowd. Keep publicizing courses so that the church knows there is always one coming up soon to which they can bring friends. Encourage members who have never brought someone to come and 'taste' how good they are. This helps overcome their fears and nerves about inviting others.

Large churches

- Don't settle for a trickle of people coming to other events and courses, just because newcomers turn up easily on Sundays. If you do, you may end up just settling at the size you are, and the church will slowly lose its evangelistic impetus. Don't let Come and See become a subdepartment for a keen few, while others get false security from large numbers at main meetings. Address the strategic importance of Christians inviting others to events so that a gospel impact can be made.

- Take a careful look at how busy your members are. Do you build in enough time for them to develop normal relationships with people all around them, the people they are going to invite to other gospel events? An overcrowded schedule may be slowly cutting off a key outreach strategy.

Discussion questions

1. Has your leadership group planned anything like this as a part of your missional strategy? Do you foster an invite mindset? If you do, you may convert some wonderful Lydias.

2. Guesstimate what percentage of Christians in your church personally invite people to events. Think of ways that you can encourage that percentage to grow – perhaps by sharing some of the information in this chapter or perhaps by some teaching on 'the inviters' mentioned in the Bible.

3. When you have encouraged people to invite friends to events, what fears, problems and challenges did you face? How did you overcome these?

4. Do you monitor the quality of the welcome to the invite events you plan? Do you encourage visitor feedback? Have leaders ever been trained in the 'as-if' principle mentioned on page 159? How well do they implement it?

5. What are your pathways so that people can be enabled to access what they need to find out for the level of interest they exhibit?

6. As a leadership, how good are you at meeting new people and following them up? Evaluate your methods of identifying, welcoming and communicating to new people, especially those who come to invite events. Does a significant percentage go relatively unnoticed?

9. TOUCH A COMMUNITY: 'CARE AND SERVE' CHANGES LIVES FOR EVER

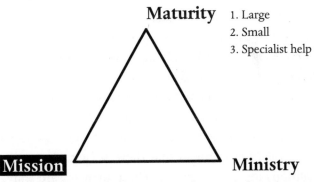

Maturity 1. Large
2. Small
3. Specialist help

Mission
1. Provide Come and See
2. Promote Care and Serve
3. Prepare for Go and Tell

Ministry
1. Organize teams
2. Train team leaders
3. Use CARE and SHAPE

Figure 9.1: Ministry map: focus on Mission: Care and Serve

What about those who aren't friends or contacts of existing members? What else should local churches be doing? Can Christians engage with the Lord's purposes for mission in other ways? You know the answer to that last question!

This chapter will explore another aspect of the mission programme described for us in the life of the early church. It will show a different approach, which will reach the people you may least expect.

The Bible encourages doing good to all, whether they convert or not (see especially Galatians 6:10). God shows his kindness to the righteous and the unrighteous (Matthew 5:45), and so should we. Acts of kindness can indeed connect people to the gospel.

When good deeds meet evil practice

After having introduced us to Lydia, a rich, religious woman converted at a meeting, Luke then shows us someone very different from her indeed (Acts 16:16–24). This person is a girl, and though she 'earned a great deal of money', it was not for herself but for her owners (Acts 16:16), for she was a slave. More dramatically, rather than being a 'worshipper of God' like Lydia (verse 14), she could not have been more dissimilar, for she was demonically possessed. She was thus enslaved in two senses, oppressed both economically and spiritually.

Timothy Keller talks about her being reached through 'Deed ministry'.[1] This doesn't mean that there wasn't a message, for the demons inside of her say, 'These men . . . are *telling* you the way to be saved' (verse 17, emphasis added). But who needs demonic endorsement? Luke emphasizes that she is reached through *compassionate action*, and an encounter between the forces of darkness and the power of God. He doesn't give us details of what else happened to her but, given the overall context of Acts 16, he is strongly indicating that such a girl is freed by Christ, much like the demoniac is freed and put into his right mind by the Saviour in Luke 8:26–39.

Luke also emphasizes two other things. Firstly, there is difference in the time scale involved. After 'many days' (verse 18), Paul acted and she was delivered. That compares and contrasts with the first time that Lydia heard and was converted. Secondly, Luke shows that such work will be costly – it cost Paul a severe beating. Vested interests will always strike back in an ugly way, using such powers as they have to twist others against the gospel, and whole communities, including the authorities, may be part of a resistance to acts of kindness done in Jesus' name (see Acts 4:8–10).

Many churches have all their eggs in the basket of getting friends to events or running meetings for them (one thinks especially of children's work), but demon-possessed slave girls aren't generally people's friends and won't get reached however good your invite culture is. You need to go and find people like this.

'Care and Serve'

Recently a couple who had been helped by similar Deed ministry got married shortly after becoming Christian believers. At the wedding, the bride's mum came up to me and said with tears in her eyes that her daughter would never have got to this place without the help of the church. She feared that self-harm or worse would have seemed the only option in the past to 'free' her from the many chains that held her. Now she could see hope, happiness and new life all in her daughter's lovely smile. Without an intentional Deed ministry, we would never even have met her.

That's what fostering a strategy of 'Care and Serve' in the community can achieve. Working deliberately to help people, believing that God may use this to set up a context in which a spiritual journey can begin, and trusting that for some it will lead to conversion, is a way forward to reach a different set of people.

Many individuals are involved in something like this – some kind of service for community well-being. Someone may be a volunteer for Meals on Wheels or hospital transport, or be a Girl Guide troop leader – the list of ways is endless (see Acts 9:36–39). Some do amazing things; I think of one man who helped down-and-outs for years at great sacrifice to himself and his family. Such service gives lots of personal opportunities to witness to Christ.

The church can also play a role in organizing community projects that do good and reach people that other gospel methods don't.

Learning about the history of the diaconate helps. In England, most deacons serve the church by carrying out such practical tasks as administration, finances and the upkeep of premises. Many diaconates in small churches also act as informal elderships to help a single full-time minister, or to lead the church when there is no full-time worker at all. This contrasts markedly with the diaconal tradition in Presbyterian churches in Scotland and the Netherlands. There, ruling elders lead the church, and the deacons are responsible for practical acts of compassion, both within *and* outside the church in the wider community.

It has been a wake-up call for people to realize that though we live in one of the most economically advanced nations on earth, the social problems resulting from human sin don't go away. Only now are these problems on such a scale that even the government can't continue to fund the help that is needed. Social commentator Peter Hitchens remarks, 'Britain cannot possibly afford its welfare state for much longer. Most people do not realize that state handouts (£207 billion a year) mop up every penny we pay in income tax (£155 billion a year).'[2] Cutbacks show the government facing up to this, but still it leaves people in the UK often, and desperately, needing help.

So, informed by all of this, we began to organize deeds of kindness and ministries of mercy in a more deliberate way. This is not middle-class paternalistic action done at a distance by well-intentioned people immunized from life's difficulties. Rather, this is being carried out by those living in the community, intentionally and in an organized way, helping those they might not otherwise know as friends.

Developing Deed ministry in a community

As a church, we have experienced some of what Luke hints at.

- *Cost*: It has taken significant resources of staff, money and energy to be allocated intentionally to reach those we would not otherwise encounter.
- *Time*: Results have been much slower than from the invite methodology mentioned before.
- *Outcome*? Wonderful! People with amazing stories of how God has saved and delivered them as they were touched by Christian kindness and gospel power.

There is so much help required that no one church can meet all its community's needs. It's good to recognize that other churches may be doing things and there is no need to duplicate. In Bedford, one church runs a counselling centre, helping with pregnancy advice. Another does a fantastic job with homeless people. Several churches administer a food bank.

We wondered what we could do, given our size (medium at the time), so we initiated a support group called 'The Net' for people from isolated and vulnerable situations. Local health-care workers were asked to refer individuals to our new group. Good relationships with local caring workers were developed, networking was diligent and high standards were maintained.

People started to come. They spread the word about the benefits of the group. Among twenty, there could easily have been twelve different nationalities at events run by a part-time staff worker with a team of church volunteers who befriended, advised and cared for children, and did crafts and other activities. In time, we allocated more resources and another part-time staff worker. An experienced fundraiser from the church volunteered time, and other members provided help such as distributing Christmas hampers.

After a couple of years, the workers were a bit worried that the church leadership would be asking, 'Where are the gospel results?' But leaders have to give this time and not be driven by a quick return. As relationships were cemented, questions and opportunities arose, which led to a few people initially, and then many, beginning the journey to faith.

Expanding our Deed ministry

Encouraged by what we saw of people, otherwise unknown to us, being reached by Deed ministry, we discovered further opportunities. For example, two deacons started giving advice to people in debt. It got beyond them. It even got beyond a financial expert whom we consulted, whose advice was to engage with the well-respected charity Christians Against Poverty (CAP). After research and negotiations, we were able to open a CAP centre in the town. The church now funds this, providing free, expert help to those trapped in debt. The manager has a team who befriend clients and provide ongoing support. Friendships have also led some on to the journey to faith. Getting people out of crippling debt is a good thing in itself and we rejoice to see God's kindness in this. To see people delivered from a greater debt, the debt of sins, is even more exciting!

Other opportunities were unsought. The headmistress of a local school asked if we could release one of our members to work with them to support needy families. She had noticed this woman was so kind to others that she wanted to extend her work. If the school and church could partner, it would be a blessing to all. The headmistress, by the way, was not a Christian believer, but a person of great goodwill, with a desire, like ours, to see the community flourish. We jointly financed this mutually beneficial venture, and the community is a better place as a result.

Others have set up an ESOL (English for Speakers of Other Languages) course. Bedford is a multicultural town with many new arrivals, for whom English is a difficult language. This free course helps them, while also helping us build relationships with them. Someone else runs lunchtime meetings for elderly people. A free lunch is followed by a thought-provoking talk, reaching people we wouldn't otherwise access.

The Care-and-Serve strategy often involves members volunteering and being supported by staff workers. Volunteers need responsibility, training, recognition and encouragement, and you can't do anything without these. The strategy gets many involved in bringing the gospel to people who have felt needs.

Connecting people to the gospel

Where does the gospel fit into all of this? Much of the time it is shared through conversations. Many people want to find out more and are given a warm invitation to church. Often when they have come and heard the gospel, they have kept coming. Those from socially disadvantaged backgrounds have found the church to be a place of acceptance and love.[3] They see true community worked out in a situation where they are welcomed. This is a message that contrasts powerfully with our highly individualized and achievement-at-all-costs culture.

One working-class man called Keith once remarked that he found it amazing that his best friend was a highly qualified research scientist whose wife was a lawyer. He could never have imagined that before becoming a Christian. Another couple, Brian and Sue, after a lifetime of problems, heard the gospel and became believers. They are learning to read, and now read the Bible. They are getting out of debt and have some money in an account, but it's never easy to manage on the little that comes in. They come to church and especially like the talks and friendship. Their health is poor though and they have to take many tablets. Their little car constantly breaks down. They still live on a tough estate and get hassle from the local yobs. But we pray with them and commit everything to our heavenly Father, and he gives them grace to cope every day. Their presence is a joy, and they love being part of the family of the living God.

For those who can't make church on Sunday, we developed a course geared for women on the fringe called the Well Woman Workshop. It covers social, physical, emotional, practical and spiritual well-being. Childcare and food are provided. Each week, a Christian woman from the church comes in to address an aspect of life. For example, a dance and fitness instructor takes the week on physical well-being; another who has struggled with anorexia will talk about caring for your mental health; a leader from the Explore course shares her story of becoming a Christian believer during the spirituality week. Lots of women have accessed this course, and many have gone on to Christianity Explored. It's another pathway in, another of the multiple entry points.

Men, as we have seen and will see in the next chapter, are a tougher nut to crack. We set up something which would directly help needy and disadvantaged men whom we wouldn't meet through normal friendships or by neighbourhood contact. It's called 'MEND: new directions for men'. We contacted local social workers and voluntary agencies, and through them men were referred to us for a course which helps them cope with life. Unlike women, guys seem to be more reluctant to complete a course and to take it further.

It is critical to have stepping stones for ministry to connect people to the gospel. Meeting real needs is where it starts. Relationships and conversations are where it goes next. And courses and church are where the gospel can be explored in more depth.

Once we got to know individuals, they could be involved in appropriate Come-and-See events, and could begin to invite people from their own social network to gospel contexts too. The two strategies are not mutually exclusive.

The church's complexion is now more reflective of the overall community. It is much more ethnically and socially diverse. This speaks powerfully to a fractured world of a power and a love that can unite people who are so very different – just as Keith found out. It makes visible Paul's statement to the Galatians: 'You are all sons of God through faith in Christ Jesus . . . There is neither Jew nor Greek, slave nor free, male nor female, for you are all one in Christ Jesus' (Galatians 3:26–28).

In multicultural, multi-ethnic and multi-religious towns like Bedford, this is a huge plus. Unity in diversity is very attractive, acting as a magnet and helping people who feel self-conscious of their background to feel that they belong.

Questions you may be asking

How much money does it all cost?
For us, this direct community work now costs the equivalent of between one and a half and two full-time workers (out of five and a half workers) in terms of time and money. There is also a discretionary budget to help those people on the brink financially, and we fund our CAP centre, which involves a significant contribution to the CAP Central HQ in Bradford. So the costs are not insignificant. But it started with just a one-day-a-week part-time worker, so not out of reach for many churches.

What about staff workers?
We have found that women, in particular, have taken our work in the community forward, establishing links with other women, networking well and advancing our evangelism efforts with women. This work would be difficult, because of time demands, even for a pastor and his wife to do. We realized that a lot of this can be done by part-time workers who can then galvanize the volunteer hours others can offer.

Paul sends greetings to a whole host of people in Romans 16, of whom many are women: 'Greet Priscilla and Aquila, my fellow-workers in Christ Jesus . . . Greet Tryphena and Tryphosa, those women who work hard in the Lord . . .' (Romans 16:3–16). Community gospel work is an area where women can serve effectively on behalf of their churches.

What other human resources does this require?

What else have we learned from adopting a Care-and-Serve strategy? A character filled with grace, for one. For you can do your very best and still see people turn away from Christianity. But never forget that doing good in the community has intrinsic value to God. You mustn't lose heart or commitment when disappointment comes your way.

We also found that at the intersection between church and community, there is a big danger that church people expect Christian behaviour from non-Christians. We have to work hard to overcome our weaknesses in this area. Fear or risk-aversion can hold Christians back from getting involved with people in need. We can wonder whether people will expect too much of us or whether we will know what to say.

We have a saying: 'Come as you are, but don't stay as you are.' We want anyone to feel warmly welcomed (remember the 'as-if' principle mentioned previously). We long to see God's grace transform lives. Yet combining patience with expectancy is a difficult balancing act.

What about church size?

Does size shape the kind of community work you can do? When we were a small church, we weren't without effective Deed ministry, but it was mainly done by individuals with church-backed prayer. But now multi-aspect community work means that many more people come into contact with the church and the gospel message than before. These people are often from social groups hard to find through normal social interaction.

Geoff Knott comments, 'Social Action seems to enable connection to people.' He goes on to say, 'Church size makes a huge difference to the effect on church growth – the larger

the church, the greater the effect. This may reflect the fact
that larger churches undertake more initiatives . . . [and] the
initiative is more fruitful.'[4]

An MP once remarked to me that he'd love to see churches
in Bedford grow to 1,000 strong, for, he said, they do so
much for the community. But he pleaded for us not to start
ten churches of 100. He had worked out the economies of
scale.

What about cooperating with others?

Care and Serve has helped our relationships with local authorities. It has put us on their radar and is looked on favourably.
Community action programmes can be done in conjunction
with official agencies in order to advance community flourishing. So, for example, the local council, its park rangers and
the charity Spurgeon's partnered with us in running an
open-air carol service in a local park.

This is obviously much easier and more effective as the
church gets larger and intentional about this strategy, but
small churches can be effective too.

What about relationships?

Care and Serve works because it builds a strong relational glue
between people. It isn't about impersonal programmes run
by bureaucrats or specialists who dip in and out of their clients'
lives. It is an investment in relationships, rather than just a
programme meeting a need. Some choose to move on from
that relationship once their need is met. Many, however, are
grateful for the relationship and want to see it deepened. The
gospel creates the deepest bond of all, and it is thrilling to see
that develop in the hearts of men and women who were once
far from God, but are now, like the slave girl, in God's family
and brothers and sisters in Christ.

Once such individuals are converted, they, as newly sent missionaries to others, begin to bring good news to those they know and live among. If people like what you do, *they* will do your publicity for you (not forgetting that if you don't do a good job, they will gossip about that too!). Previous client stories are one of the most powerful weapons in relaying the gospel. Spoken or even unspoken, people notice and wonder that God is amazing.

Final thought: where would we be without converted 'slave girls' in heaven? Or in the church? If you are going to meet them and see them delivered from oppression, it's worth realizing that it needs intentionality and costly intervention in some kind of Care-and-Serve strategy. What is yours going to be?

Growth suggestions for churches of different sizes

Small churches

- Build on what individual members are already doing. A Girl Guide leader, for example, will inevitably come into contact with many needy girls from complex family backgrounds. Your church could pray regularly for her ministry.
- Collect items and money to make up Christmas hampers. Deliver them to individuals whom members know who are needy or neglected.

Medium-sized churches

- There are Christian para-church organizations which value cooperating with churches in Deed ministry.

This will introduce a medium-sized church into new possibilities in the future. For example, a church could support Christian work in prisons.

- More directly, a medium-sized church could join an already established programme and partner with it, helping a food-bank system.
- Offer courses that address people's felt needs: 'How to drug-proof your kids', parenting skills, marriage preparation and divorce recovery help build credibility and develop relationships in the community.

Awkward-sized churches

- Begin to build relationships with local agencies. Capitalize on the church's growing visibility to establish networks with other service providers. This not only enables the church to be better informed about needs, but also builds confidence with agencies.
- Encourage the whole church to pray for Deed ministry, even if each individual can't be personally committed to every project.

Large churches

- Develop a few projects really well. The needs are huge, and the temptation is to respond to every request that comes your way or to develop ministries reflecting every burden the members feel. Better to be a small-but-effective part of all that is happening than to gain a reputation for doing lots but of poor-quality stuff.
- Don't disconnect Word and Deed, but remember that Word needs accessing in a variety of ways. Low-key discussions while relaxing may be a better way for some

men to access Christian truth than a direct 'Here's-what-you-have-to-learn' course. Keep making sure that Deed and Word go together, for another temptation for the large church is not to think about this, but just to organize deeds, because there is always a crowd under the Word of God on a Sunday.

Discussion questions

1. Do you know what Deed ministries your members are involved with in their personal lives? Could the church/ home group pray more thoughtfully about these?
2. Have you ever done a local audit of what people in your area require most help with and who may already be meeting some of those needs?
3. Do you look at the input and output of Deed ministry? If you put little in, you will get little out. But even if you are putting resources in, is there enough joined-up thinking and a clear pathway for people to connect to the gospel in ways that help them? A disconnect of deeds and words may lead to few disciples being made – is that what you are finding?
4. Discuss the spiritual and sociological struggles that: (a) outside people face as they are reached by Deed ministry; and (b) many Christians face as those very different from themselves come into the orbit of church life.

10. TRANSFORM A LIFE: PREPARING EVERYONE FOR 'GO AND TELL'

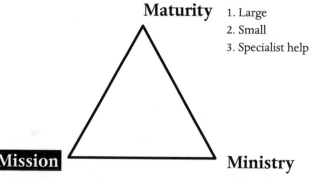

Maturity	1. Large
	2. Small
	3. Specialist help

Mission	Ministry
1. Provide Come and See	1. Organize teams
2. Promote Care and Serve	2. Train team leaders
3. Prepare for Go and Tell	3. Use CARE and SHAPE

Figure 10.1: Ministry map: focus on Mission: Go and Tell

Heaven had mounted a Search-and-Rescue mission, and I hadn't quite grasped how much I was part of it until the phone rang late one Saturday night. Preparation for the next day's talks was put aside, as I had to be ready for what would develop in the next couple of hours.

Roger had been due to fly to the USA, except he was too petrified to go. A terrorist incident and threats of reprisals to aircraft left him anxious about life . . . and what was beyond death. Desperately, he had driven round looking for churches. He popped in on one; nobody there. But he had cried out in his heart, 'God, if you are there, help me!' A series of contacts led to my name coming up as a pastor in his town.

All day long, he had been putting off the decision. He needed to talk to someone *right now*. As I entered the house, he was sitting, head in hands, being comforted by his wife, Sarah, who was, frankly, very sceptical about my presence. How could I talk to both of them in their differing circumstances? I knew the gospel could overcome all kinds of obstacles, but now I, and it, were being put to the kind of test only reality can bring. And so we began to talk . . .

Talking progressed until both, during the next few months, became Christians. Perhaps surprisingly, Sarah came to faith first during a message from 1 Peter 2:10: '. . . but now you have received mercy.' She confessed her new-found trust in Christ. I remember it well. Roger came to a gradual assurance of God's grace in Jesus. The gospel had passed the test. I suppose I had too, even if inadequate was how I felt. I was glad, though, that God had prepared me to 'Go and Tell'.

Church growth must never be about tinkling with mere numbers. As we read the slow-motion replay in the Bible of how God touches lives, it's so that we can be ready for the high-speed drama in which the Spirit will involve us.

This is undoubtedly so in the passage shaping us, and reaching people far from God is at the heart of this book. We have considered two of the converts in Acts 16 and seen how different they were. There is one more story to tell. From all this, we will see that churches can develop three distinct, but not unconnected, means of impacting a community and reaping gospel fruit.

Man to man

The final story in Acts shows us a man saved through coming into contact with other men who explained the gospel to him. Who was he? How was he reached?

Who was he?

This man, a jailer, was doing a civil service job, in all likelihood a nice little earner, for a retired Roman legionary. He was a family man, with children growing up. He had no obvious interest in Christianity, as he locked up his prisoners just as he would any charged to him. Perhaps he was cruel to them, taking his cue from the way the authorities had treated them, for they had been 'thrown into prison'. He made sure they were 'in the inner cell' and he 'fastened their feet in the stocks' (Acts 16:23–24). This form of torture would have added to their pain at being 'severely flogged' (verse 23).

The most important thing we learn about him, however, is that he is a man of honour. Recall what the soldiers say to one another in the 2000 film *Gladiator* as they prepare for battle against barbarian hordes: 'Strength and honour'. This is his world, the world of many men, a world where personal honour comes before other spiritual and moral concerns. It sets the standards by which to live and die. It's rooted in a strong desire for the approval of others. This man wants to be respected by his peers. Without that, life isn't worth living. There are many men like him.

This all surfaces when he wakes up after a mighty earth-quake. He sees open doors and assumes the prisoners have taken their chance to escape. For him, this is no mere mishap, but points to a dereliction of duty. He cannot bear to live with the shame that he has let down those above and around him, that he has failed as a man. He'd rather end his life honourably and bring pain on his family, than bring dishonour upon himself and them. He is not a coward taking an easy way out, but a man of 'strength and honour' for whom honour leaves him only one option. He is about to kill himself when he hears a voice from a man unlike any other man he has ever met.

How was he reached?

Any Roman soldier would have mixed with plenty of courageous men. But this one had never met prisoners who could cope with such a beating and then remain calm in an earthquake and not take the opportunity to escape. The other prisoners hadn't escaped either. They had heard Paul and Silas singing songs of praise to God around midnight, and when the earthquake came, instead of running as fast as they could, they were transfixed, even though their chains had come loose and their cell doors were flung open wide. Trembling as he might, at such a power as he has never encountered before, the Roman asks the now-famous question: 'Sirs, what must I do to be saved?' (verse 30).

How revealing is that? Even *in extremis* and left to ourselves, we are creatures of inveterate works righteousness. We want *to do something* to save ourselves, earn our way, deserve our acceptance and gain God's approval.

What he was given was the gospel of grace. He was told, in effect, 'You don't need to "do" anything; it has already been "done" for you. You only have to "believe" (trust in / depend / rely) on another.' That other? The crucified Saviour Jesus Christ. Salvation had been *achieved* by him so that it could be *received* by us.

Why could Paul and Silas sing praise songs while blood congealed on their painful wounds? Because another's wounds had brought them the deeper healing of their souls. As Peter puts it:

> When they hurled their insults at him, he did not retaliate; when he suffered, he made no threats. Instead, he entrusted himself to him who judges justly. He himself bore our sins in his body on the tree, so that we might die to sins and live for righteousness; by his wounds you have been healed.
>
> (1 Peter 2:23–24)

Paul and Silas have good news for men brought to the end of themselves, and they share it freely with their tormentor 'at that hour of the night' (verse 33). He and his whole household believe and are baptized as a sign of a new relationship with God. Another great marker showing that a transformation had taken place was his willingness to be hospitable; what a great sign that is of changed relationships. A popular worship song talks about once being an enemy, but now seated at the Lord's Table. If we have experienced coming to his table, we will want others to sit at our table too. We leave the jailer and his whole family filled with joy. How good is that?

Go-and-Tell principles

The situation is unique, but the lessons are abiding. This helps develop a third strategy: 'Go and Tell'. Three principles inform that, one of which I'll discuss briefly, two at greater length.

Keep close to God
Having gone to Europe to tell the gospel, the apostle Paul found himself in a situation where he had the opportunity to

share the faith. He showed great grace to a man who caused him great pain. To do that, he needed to keep close to God himself. That's why he was singing songs of praise in the night. He had 'kept himself in God's love' (see Jude 21). In his book, *Becoming a Contagious Christian*, Bill Hybels highlights the importance of 'salt being salty' (see Matthew 5:13). He talks about HP – High Potency – if we are to be useful in the Lord's service.[1]

Keep close to people
Our lives also need to be in loving contact with the lives of others. The apostle Paul may have had no choice about being near the jailer in the prison, but he could have chosen how to react – in love, with indifference, or even hatred. What a difference his choice made.

Most of us have the privilege of making choices that can make a difference too. Work, home, leisure, neighbourhood and family give us lots of people we can choose to mix with. They all watch and notice. Sadly, many Christians lose the sense that they know lots of people far from God or don't think that God will use them to touch others' lives. Over time, they lose loving contact with people far from God. The following diagram says it all.

Number of friends I have far from God

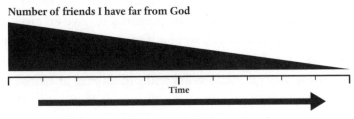

Figure 10.2: Number of friends I have far from God

Many Christians were once taught that having no non-Christian friends was a goal to aim for – ultimate sanctification!

In her helpful book, *Out of the Saltshaker*, Becky Manley-Pippert points out that it's no good having pristine salt in an admired saltshaker. It's got to be mixed in with the food. So too we need to be up close and personal if we are to help people. Hybels characterizes this as CP (Close Proximity). Paul certainly had that.[2]

Why estrangement happens
Many believers begin to spend more and more time with other Christians. Churches of all sizes can draw them into an increasingly crowded programme, gobbling up all their discretionary time, so that there's little left over for relationships with people far from God, or they don't think the ones they already have are of interest to the Lord. Churches can set up programmes at which the majority of attendees are believers with just a sprinkling of non-Christians. Think of church football teams, church hobby clubs, for example.

It may also be true that, as we age, we become more conservative and settled in our pattern of living, and hence our circle of acquaintanceships doesn't change much. If this is added to the church busyness factor, then the arrow of time can be a real threat to Close Proximity. We settle for an attitude that says, 'They realize I am a Christian, and if they want to know more, they know whom to ask.' We may hide behind 1 Peter 3:15: 'Always be prepared to give an answer to everyone who asks you to give a reason for the hope that you have.' We think, 'Well, I would answer, *but no-one asks*', and so we may go many years without talking of Christ to other people.

The Master wants us mixed in and making a difference: 'My prayer is not that you take them out of the world but that you protect them from the evil one' (John 17:15). Paul tells Christians in Corinth, 'I have written to you in my letter not to associate with sexually immoral people – *not at all meaning the people of this world* who are immoral, or the greedy and swindlers, or idolaters. In that case you would have to leave this world. But now I am writing to you that you must not associate with anyone who calls himself a brother but who is sexually immoral . . .' (1 Corinthians 5:9–11, emphasis added).

Getting alongside outsiders

To counter these tendencies, get intentional about proximity to others. Explore 'space' to overcome the problems of time. The grid below looks at four areas where Christians could meet non-Christians if they just think about it. Put names in that grid, and it will soon add up to a long list of people *you actually know*. Your problem is that you have stopped thinking that God could change their lives.

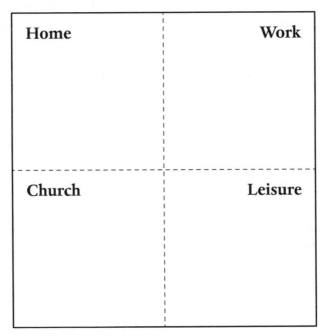

Figure 10.3: Home, work, church and leisure

Here in Acts 16, Luke presents us with the human impossibility of a tough man being reached for Christ. It reminds us that 'all things are possible with God' (Mark 10:27). The Lord wants our availability. We can explore relationships all around us which are already there, or could be there with a little effort. Work is a classic, for most of us meet people in the course of our work. We don't have to learn a language or change our clothing as many missionaries to other cultures do; all that adaptation is already working for us. We need to see ourselves as full-time Christian workers placed by a loving God in our situations.

A choice you can make
What will it take for this to develop more positively in your life? First and foremost, you need to make *intentional choices* to be where other people are. You can do this especially with your discretionary and leisure time, and at work you can make decisions to be alongside others rather than be alone.

In the loft, I have a boxed-up model railway. It would be perfectly legitimate (though a bit 'anoraky'?) to build it. One day, this may be the best thing to do with my time and money. Having grandchildren is a useful added justification. Yet right now, I choose to spend spare time playing sport. You should see the team! Average age sixty, me part of the team's youth strategy (at fifty-six), most of us crocked up from injuries sustained years ago. But still competing against teams a third our age. The team is full of characters, and we are all good friends. These are guys I pray for. I try to be available to God to point these men to the Saviour of the world.

I am certainly not saying you can't have, or don't need, personal time alone. It will, nevertheless, take intentional choices to do something *where other people are*. Bill Hybels is one of the world's great Christian leaders and communicators.

Yet he confessed to being disappointed with his 'batting average' when it came to personal evangelism. Looking back on those people God had used him to touch, he realized there was a common thread. What was it? The willingness to walk across a room, greet someone and show concern for their lives.[3] You and I can do that; that's where some Close Proximity starts. So next time a new neighbour moves in, next time there is a bereaved person in your street or at work, next time someone celebrates the birth of a child or grandchild, or even their sports team winning something, show some human interest and trust that God will use you to touch a life.

Start by letting others know (in a wise way) you are a Christian. Ask them about their own ideas about life as opportunities arise. Listen to their challenges and offer to pray for them. You may be able to share some of the stresses you face and how trusting in God helps you. It's in this context that gospel conversations can develop.[4]

Dave Bennett found that many were led to consider Christianity because of some crisis in their lives (77% of females and 53% of males); this included 12% recently bereaved, 12% facing an illness and 21% dealing with a family issue. Being sensitive to the needs of others and willing to help was important. The church can't organize this; it is up to individual Christians to serve God by serving their neighbour. Close Proximity is especially important at a time when things go wrong. If 'man is born to trouble as surely as sparks fly upward' (Job 5:7), then it is only a matter of time before those we know will need help. All of us are only a day away from our comfort being shaken, and our need of grace being uncovered. The jailer was. So too are the people around you.

Bennett comments, 'The stories . . . were examined to see who took the first action in the process of them coming to faith. In 165 out of the 383, the first action was taken by an *individual* Christian.' Many of these, as with the jailer, were challenged by lifestyle: 'In the list of 22 topics which could have influenced them becoming a Christian the lifestyle of a Christian *came first for males* and ninth for females.' One man wrote about what had influenced him: '. . . by being my friend and living the life of a Christian. Her life was the Bible I used to read.'[5]

Keep close to God; keep close to people. Now for the third and crucial principle.

Speak to people for God

You can put closeness to God and closeness to people together, and what do you get as a result? *People still far away from God.* Why? Because the gospel is a message that has to be communicated. It is *good news* of what God has done, the victory over our worst enemies which any of us can enter into and benefit from, when we hear and believe.

Paul logically and eloquently says,

> [The] Lord . . . richly blesses all who call on him, for 'Everyone who calls on the name of the Lord will be saved.' How, then, can they call on the one they have not believed in? And how can they believe in the one of whom they have not heard? And how can they hear without someone preaching to them? And how can they preach unless they are sent? As it is written, 'How beautiful are the feet of those who bring good news!'
> (Romans 10:11–15)

If non-Christians only see your life, but don't hear the message, they think, 'You are a good person and you are religious. I guess you want me to become religious like you and try to be a better person. OK, I'll try to be more religious.' Or they might think, 'I am a good person and I am like you, except you are religious and I am not. I can't see that the religious bit is that important.' Or even: 'Why would I want to become religious like you? I am quite all right as I am, even though I am going through a difficult patch just now.'

Speaking clearly for God
People assume there are two ways to live: 'the irreligious way' and 'the religious way'. In one, you keep God at arm's length; in the other, you try to be a better person by being religious so that you gain acceptance with God and merit his blessings by your commitment. That's natural reasoning. People need *to hear that the gospel is something entirely different,* a third way that can help both the religious, like Lydia, to be freed from duty that will never put her heart at peace, and the irreligious, like the jailer, who can't imagine grace until someone explains it to him.

When the message (what Hybels calls Clear Communication), gets combined with High Potency and Close Proximity, then, by God's grace, comes the powerful change of conversion. Hybels' way of putting it is: HP + CP + CC = MI (Maximum Impact).[6] Slightly cringey but neat, memorable – and *important.*

Why? Many Christians stumble at just this point. Giving some kind of verbal witness is the time when they feel they let God down the most. It is not a sin of commission (doing something wrong), but the sin of omission (not doing what's right). Sometimes life brings difficulties which allow conversations to spark. We can take the cowardly way out or the courageous way in. Many of us have ducked out when we could have spoken up.

It's in this area that believers need help, encouragement and training. If you, as a leadership team, *provide* Come and See by organizing good events, and if you *promote* Care and Serve in the community, you need to *prepare* Christians for Go and Tell, whatever size church you are.

How prepared are your members to communicate the faith? We may assume that if they have heard lots of sermons they will be able to share. Wrong. I recall training in sharing one's personal faith story ('Simply, in two minutes, using no jargon, tell the person next to you the essence of how you become a Christian'). A lovely Christian said she would not know where to start, and would be too embarrassed even telling her nearest and dearest. Yet she had heard thousands of sermons!

Preparing for Go and Tell

Many leaders assume that rallying cries will do the job. We have found, however, that we needed:

1. to be more thoughtful, addressing people's fears and anxieties;
2. to impart some ready-to-hand skills to call on when opportunities arise; and
3. to give people practice so they realize that speaking for Jesus isn't impossible.

The word 'evangelism' has a certain feel about it. Becky Manley-Pippert grew up with it ringing in her ears, but it had a negative tone. She writes, 'Christians and non-Christians have something in common: we're both uptight about evangelism. Our fear as Christians seems to be: *How many people have I offended this week?* We think we must be a little obnoxious in order to be good evangelists. A tension builds inside: *Should I be sensitive to people and forget about evangelism or should I blast them with the gospel and forget about their dignity as human beings?'* She goes on to say, 'There was a part of me that secretly felt evangelism was something you shouldn't do to your dog, let alone a friend.'[7] Ever felt something similar?

Tools you can use

To counter this common feeling, utilize helpful tools. One is called 'The Evangelism Styles Questionnaire'.[8] Answers are self-scored, totals added up and patterns emerge. It's not a scientific assessment; it aims to show we have different personality characteristics when it comes to sharing our faith. The final profiles use six characteristics, each one equated to someone used by God in the Bible to bring the gospel to others. So Peter is the prime example of being direct, Paul is the intellectual type, Barnabas has interpersonal skills, and so forth. God has made us with our own personalities; gladly embrace that and work with the grain of who you are. Trust God to use you to bring good news to others in ways that work with your personality.

For many, that comes as a welcome surprise. I, for one, needed to hear it. I am a classic introvert, a shy person who finds meeting strangers a challenge. When I became a Christian, impersonal forms of evangelism were still the favoured outreach method. I joined my church's door-to-door programme and used to wish people were out as I walked up the path to the door. If someone was brusque, I found myself squirming. Years later, when I knocked on doors to get customers for my window-cleaning business, I was equally nervous, and they could be equally rude. However, I realized that it's not necessarily a reaction to Christianity but a 'Please-stop-disturbing-me!' reaction.

This questionnaire was distributed to our members. We are talking Brits here, and many hated the idea but nevertheless

completed it. Why do it as a whole group? The good reason
was that, when hands started going up to indicate which style
was the dominant one, everyone could see that across the
church we had a good spread of styles. We could see, 'We are
on a team' in this. The exercise helped us not to worry about
what we were not, as God had placed each part in the body
to do what he wanted in evangelism, as in other things.

Sometimes we feel useless because we are not what
someone else is. Many men of the quiet-but-strong type,
seeing articulate communicators up front, feel that they are
therefore not the kind of person God uses. All could see that
each individual could be used and we all worked together on
Go and Tell.

Telling the gospel

Yet we hadn't actually quite got to speaking the gospel with
this tool. We offered some more help: one form was learning
to tell 'your story', and the other was learning to tell 'his
story'.

Sometimes we get the opportunity to share our own
personal journey of life, and coming to faith is a key part
of that. Non-Christians often love to tell their stories if we
ask, and our first skill is learning to be an active listener.
In that context, there may be an opportunity to tell your
story too.

Can you? Some begin a bit like this: 'Well, it was sometime
in 1993, no, it may have been '94 . . . or could it have been '95,
when I was washed in the blood . . .' The story is either
rambling and dull or full of subcultural Christian-speak. True
but obscure. We wanted to help people by training them to
come up with a clear and concise version of their own story.
To facilitate this, one member offered to vet each person's
story of coming to faith using understandable language and

deliverable in two minutes. Rarely do you get two hours, so why not practise for the shorter version? Anyone can pad it out!

We encouraged a 'before, during and after' outline, much as Paul employs. (Luke emphasizes Paul's story three times utilizing this structure – see Acts 9:1–19; 22:1–21; 26:1–23.) Here's mine, after my friend Bruce kindly offered feedback:

> I have always been an inquisitive person but was brought up without a religious background. A friend at school lent me a book about Christianity. It explained how we are all far away from a relationship with God. But it went on to show that God has removed the barrier of human rebellion by taking the blame himself. When Jesus died on the cross and rose again from the dead, that was what was happening. I found that this really made sense not only of my life, but of the wider world too. I took to heart what I read and became a Christian. I now enjoy listening to other people's questions and showing them how the good news of Jesus can help them.

A total of 123 words, under two minutes; I am sure you could do the same. You don't have to memorize your story verbatim, but it is useful to have the bare bones to recall.

Why sharing your story matters

God can take a prepared Christian's conversation a long way. Dave Bennett found that 46% of his sample had a Christian friend who had shared how they had become a believer; a further 17% had a Christian relative who did, and 11% heard a stranger's conversion story (that is, *nearly three-quarters* heard conversion stories before they converted). Someone sharing their story rated *second* out of the twenty-two factors which might have influenced them in becoming a Christian. This is massive! It's worth putting the effort into being as clear and helpful as possible.

Church leaders are missing a trick if they don't facilitate this. It's not about producing an airbrushed 'photoshop' product, but about giving believers freedom to tell their story with greater confidence.

Presenting his story

Sharing 'his story' can be done in a variety of ways. One of the most helpful is to teach the difference between Christianity and religion.

'How do you spell religion?'

'R . . . e . . . l . . .'

'No, you spell it: D O!'

All the world's religions teach their followers to *do* something. Some may be very specific and prescribed, while others will be relaxed and informal, but it's all about what you have to do to achieve what you want (say, peace in this life or the next).

'How do you spell Christianity?'

'D O N E'.

It's about what God has done to put you right with himself. He has come to take the blame himself and offer you reconciliation, free forgiveness and a new relationship. There is nothing else like this. Nothing.

This prepares Christians with a useful way forward in any discussion about religion or about Christianity being the only way or about people being good enough for God. It's easy to grasp, and the youngest believer can employ it.

For visual learners

What about the well-known 'bridge diagram'? Have you taught it? It has its weaknesses, as do all short summaries of the gospel. But why is it useful? Because some people are visual learners. Our eldest son has been doodling since he was a toddler. He went to art college and completed a degree in graphics with advertising. He is now a designer in a creative industry. How was he converted? He had heard the gospel since we could talk to him. Yet it was when he was fifteen, as this diagram was being drawn and explained at a church service, that God used it to bring him to faith. It happened to a deacon's son too. He is also in the art world, just completing a fine arts degree in London. He too was converted as he saw the diagram unfold. God used this presentation to help someone with that skill-set and learning style. I am not saying that the picture fully, or on its own, communicates the gospel, but it helps reinforce the words.[9]

The gospel story can be drawn in other ways too. The three crosses is a simple example: a black cross, a white one and another black, representing the thief, Jesus (the only perfectly good man who has ever lived) and the other thief. During the crucifixion, one thief had a change of heart, turned to Jesus

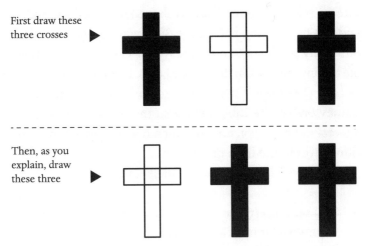

Figure 10.4: Presenting the gospel as the story of three crosses

for help and mercy and he was promised forgiveness and heaven. How could that be? Now draw a white cross and two black ones: one representing the unrepentant thief, one representing Jesus taking the blame, and the white one representing the thief who is treated as if he is the obedient son whose home is heaven. The gospel at its heart is about substitution, and this pictures it powerfully. The challenge is to ask, 'Which cross is yours?' The good news is that Jesus, the Son of God, was willing to die 'on their cross' if they will turn to him, as one of the thieves did. The promise Jesus made to him on that day is the promise he makes to any and all who turn to him.

This is useful to have ready. It gives confidence to Christians to share their faith.

Reading the Bible's story

Sharing the Bible is very helpful. The London-based evangelist, Rico Tice, urges Christians to offer to read and discuss the Bible with someone in short bursts, the whole thing taking no more than fifteen minutes, and repeated regularly. He believes that this is a great way forward for our times; I am sure he is right. Bennett found that 66% of his respondents said that being given part of the Bible was significant to them. But many get lost once they start, especially if they start at the beginning (as you do, and as I did). Unbelievers need help to read the Bible.[10] It's crucial today to communicate the framework of the Bible's story so that people can begin to understand its big picture and then make sense of their individual lives in the light of it.

One very helpful outline is called 'Take 5!':

1. God set it up (Genesis 1 – 2).
2. We messed it up (Genesis 3).
3. God calls us back (Genesis 4 – Malachi).

4. God came himself (Matthew – John).
5. What if I follow? God grows relationships (Acts – Jude).
   What if I don't follow? God will sort evil out (Revelation).

People are not machines working on automatic, but all the above gospel presentations are forms of mental muscle memory which, when mastered, will give structure and direction.

The above are also in no way a replacement for 'honest answers to honest questions', as Francis Schaeffer used to say. They aren't a quick fix or a substitute for careful listening, hard thought and serious discussion. They are just intended to help us to be able to say something useful in the moments we get.

Go and Tell in practice, *and in real life*

It is worth considering some kind of practice run. Get new members to share their story at an induction day or when they are baptized or transfer their membership to your church. Practise these simple gospel explanations every now and then. We probably don't do enough here, and believers soon forget unless they rehearse. Ironically, we demand more practice for those learning to drive than for those telling the good news of salvation – where the outcomes have eternal consequences.

This is critical. Remember, 76% of Bennett's sample said that having the gospel explained by a Christian had some significance in them becoming believers themselves. Of those, *more* people said that an *individual* explaining the gospel was significant than those who said that a public speaker was.

Bedford's most famous son is John Bunyan. He had a protracted journey to faith. What really shook him up, and helped him a great deal, is described in these words:

Upon a day, the good providence of God did cast me to Bedford to work my calling; and in one of the streets of that town, I came where there were three or four poor women sitting at a door in the sun, and talking about the things of God . . . I drew near to hear what they said . . .

He continues:

Their talk was about a new birth, the work of God on their hearts, also how they were convinced of their miserable state by nature; they talked how God had visited their souls with his love in the Lord Jesus, and with what words and promises they had been refreshed, comforted and supported against the temptations of the devil . . . [I thought] they spoke as if joy did make them speak . . . they were to me as if they had found a new world.[11]

Such personal talking about Jesus was what led Bunyan to seek out another individual, Pastor John Gifford, and through his good offices, the Lord gave Bunyan an experience of new birth and salvation. That led to one of the most widely read books after the Bible: *Pilgrim's Progress*. And all because it was sunny one morning and some nameless women, who could have been talking about the weather on their doorsteps, were talking about Christ. What an example of Go and Tell!

The long and winding road

Each conversion story is a testimony to one thing: the wonderful love of God.

Yet stories have other elements, such as the people God used to help us, what we heard and when we heard it, what helped us and what hindered; the 'Sloughs of Despond', the

'Hill Difficulty' and the 'House Beautiful' (to use Bunyan's allegorical language). When we listen to these elements, something emerges: most people's journeys, when they start as adults far from God, *take time*. From initial interest to saving faith may easily be a ten-year hike or more. The journey from 0 to 10 is rarely very quick. Bill Hybels describes something similar in the 'Just Walk across the Room' course.

Real-life stories
Three contemporary stories of people known to me illustrate the above.

One of my wife's friends, Gina, met at playgroup and school gate, encouragingly came to a carol service (though no other services), and then discouragingly she missed them for a couple of years. She then came to some autumn suppers, and before the first one she ate at home beforehand on the assumption that, as it was a Christian thing, there would be quiche and a cup of tea! Eventually, she started attending church and then came to faith. When I asked her what it was that had challenged her, she said, 'You know, what that man said.' 'Which man?' I asked. It turned out to be the preacher and pastor from Guildford, John Benton, who had spoken at the supper she had first attended *seven years earlier*. She remembered virtually every word; I had forgotten he had even been (apologies, John!). The Word had been working away in her heart, but it was years later when she truly believed it.

Now here's the story of a woman on an even longer journey. My wife met Lucy at antenatal classes when they were both expecting their first babies. A friendship developed, especially as our children met and played together regularly. Our friend had a number of ups and downs: her back was injured at work, and the loss of earnings put her under financial pressure. Her marriage dissolved, albeit amicably, leaving her with three young children to bring up. She then had to spend time in hospital with mental health issues. She came to some church things – for a while. She talked about the gospel – for a while. She read lots of books about Christianity, but she seemed to go further away than ever. At long last, after we and other Christians had prayed for her and maintained a caring friendship, she believed and was baptized. Our son, the one in the womb when the mothers had met, was by now twenty-two!

The final story is about a man called Tony. His kids came to a club we ran and were my sons' friends at school. He used to fix my car. We'd chat pleasantly when he did the (never-ending) work on the string of ageing Fiats I had (Fix It Again, Tony). One evening, as if from nowhere, he asked me a very significant question about his life. Things were playing on his mind, and he didn't know where to turn as problems developed. Sadly, his marriage broke down and he became a single dad. But church attendance and a seeker course followed, and then, one evening in my front room, the truth of the gospel dawned on him. He had to rely on what Christ had done, not try to be a better person to gain acceptance with God. He believed the gospel, and I had the privilege of taking his baptism, and his subsequent and happy new marriage. His journey from meeting me to conversion was over ten years. In his kindness, he still fixes my cars (Vauxhalls now!).

Hang on in there

We long for the day when many come to faith, deeply and quickly. Yet we must not despise a day of small (or slow) things.

If pastors move on quickly from church to church, they may be a part of someone's journey, but they won't, in all likelihood, be personally leading their own new friends to faith as a model to other believers, for that is likely to take longer than their stay in one place.

Young and new churches must learn this. They may grow fast to start with, but much of this may be recycled Christian growth. Genuine conversion growth, even in a new enthusiastic plant, may take time. The church plant has to recognize that for it to be used by God to bring new adult converts to faith, it has to be there for the long haul. This realization often kicks in just when the first flush of enthusiasm is draining, perhaps when a founding leader is moving on, and when things begin to feel not as exhilarating as in the first few years. It's then that mature leadership needs to steer the church well and keep it on a gospel course.

It's good to acknowledge that we are links in a chain and God calls us to trust him to put that whole chain together. We may be the first link, or a link away from the last, in a conversion journey. It is all about doing what we can where we are. That's where the stories of Acts 16 are so encouraging; they give us strong pointers that if we do 'God's work, God's way', we can trust him to bring people we know and love to himself.

Preparing Christians to share their faith – the 'Go and Tell' strategy – feels less well-defined. Unlike 'Come and See' and 'Care and Serve', which the church can organize centrally, this is left to each believer, wherever they are on their frontline every day. We never see all that goes on. But heaven will tell how conversations were used by the Spirit to move people towards faith.

Add up the strategies developed from the stories in Acts 16 to the two other goals of growing to maturity and serving one another in ministry, and the result is the founding of thriving gospel churches like that at Philippi. No wonder Paul said, 'I thank my God every time I remember you. In all my prayers for all of you, I always pray with joy because of your partnership in the gospel from the first day until now' (Philippians 1:3–5). Do you pray like that for your church? I hope you can soon begin to do so.

Growth suggestions for churches of different sizes

Small churches

- Get people to share regularly the names of people they already know, so that the whole church can intercede for other people.
- Get each person to write down and share with everyone else a two-minute account of how they became a believer, and pray for opportunities that someone will be given an opportunity to speak 'for real'.

Medium churches

- Utilize 'The Evangelism Styles Questionnaire' as a group experience. Encourage discussion about the different styles and how individuals identify with them. Encourage honesty about what problems are faced in personally sharing faith.
- Teach, and keep revisiting, a couple of simple gospel presentations, again as a group experience. Get people to rehearse, and encourage feedback and practice until they are done well. Then pray as a whole group that God will use you to pass this on to those who really need to hear them.

Awkward-sized churches

- Encourage all to realize that they are on the 'frontline' in their everyday lives. Church on Sunday is like a half-time team talk where Christians get refreshed to go out and make a difference in the second half/new week. To further facilitate this, get each home-group member to share the name of the boss, line manager or authority figure they have to relate to. Then keep praying for these significant people. Remember how Naaman's maid had an eternal effect on her master!

- Rehearse gospel-sharing skills in a variety of forums. Utilize great courses, such as 'Life on the Frontline' or 'Just Walk across the Room', in home groups.[12] Invest in the participants' resources that accompany these courses and make the most of them. Keep underlining how important a personal sharing of the faith is, and don't let members fall into the trap of thinking, 'Our speakers do it for us on Sundays.'

Large churches

- Make the most of special events where stories can be told. At baptisms and confirmations, or when new people join, make the most of their story. Use video technology: a live voice is very appealing. But unless someone is very capable or a trained public speaker, their great story may get lost due to poor communication techniques. To a large crowd, they may just seem a distant little figure not coming across very well, whereas if they are filmed and the editing is good, then when that story is seen on a big screen, it can be powerful. You don't need expensive studios, just the best skills you have, and do it thoughtfully.

- Offer lots of one-to-one training to empower as many as possible to get involved in communicating the faith this way. Deploy some of your best people into working with seekers and the confused. Get them to share with the whole church the benefits of spreading the gospel this way. Seek to recruit many others into learning how to do this naturally and well.

Discussion questions

1. Have you trained people in sharing their own conversion story? How could you do it in ways that don't intimidate them?

2. Have you ever got people practising simple ways of sharing the gospel story? What barriers have to be overcome in believers' minds for 'Go and Tell' to actually happen? How could you address these more effectively?

3. Have you forums where believers can share regularly with others about the opportunities God gives them to talk about Christ? Do you give any special encouragement to those on the frontline of home and work by the way you shape Sunday meetings and messages?

4. Do you ever interview people about their conversion stories in Sunday meetings? What are the pluses and minuses of doing this? How can you ensure that the downsides don't ruin the very big positives?

11. GET READY TO GROW: THE CHURCH BECOMING MISSIONAL

So, finally, we come to draw everything together, to underscore the key things and to be sent on our way, encouraged to be part of all that our amazing God is doing. Let's visit the athletics stadium, just as the starting pistol is being raised.

On your marks

The gospel of Christ has passed to us. Believing it has brought unimaginable love, peace and joy. It has delivered on its promise: the forgiveness of our sins and the indwelling of the Spirit as the guarantor of all that is to come. It's now our turn to pass it, intact, to others. Churches will start, grow and prosper. We have seen that they will require leadership. What were the big pointers to what leaders will require?

Firstly, we will need to 'ask for wisdom for the task', just as Solomon did. It is only a prayer away (James 1:5–8). Relief!

Secondly, we need to gain skills while character is being formed. When blended together, many of the challenges facing the church can be surmounted. Personal humility must be tied to a determination to see the task through. Surely we can all aspire to that?

Thirdly, we need power, but not as this world knows it, to accomplish God's will on earth. Personal weakness, leading to a humble, prayerful dependence on the One whose power can't be tyrannical is the only safe way for churches to grow and not become insufferably arrogant. Faith will evidence itself in this way.

Fourthly, we need grace, to love our world in the way God does. In all its unbelief, proud self-absorption, deliberate disobedience and self-destructive tendencies. Following the Master will involve seeing yourself and others through the eyes of Jesus, and building churches which reflect him.[1] Only as the gospel grips our own hearts will we have the motivation to stick at the challenge and winsomely proclaim Christ.

Armed with those personal leadership qualities, churches cannot but be beneficiaries. They will be nearly ready to grow. So what else have we learned that they will they need?

Getting ready . . .

Lesson number one is that churches must see themselves as missional to the UK culture. Growing a church through various size barriers is not about a competition with others, nor a badge of achievement. It is about Christ's honour, and people being transformed by the gospel.

So churches need to equip each of their members as whole-of-life disciples to live each and all day for their Lord on their frontlines. They will need to mature in their faith, to serve and to reach out with the message of life.

We know that there is a great deal of help available to enable us to grow and to work obediently for Christ. We have seen, though, that many Christians and most churches feel they struggle with reaching outsiders effectively.

We need to be Christians who, like Paul, bend over backwards yet without sinning, to win the lost for Christ (1 Corinthians 9:19–23). Many churches have made some kind of transformation in their thinking about all of this, but there is still a long way to go.[2]

The second lesson is to recall that 'the local church is the hope of the world',[3] and it is crucial that they thrive. We have been discussing ways to make the local church strong, how it can overcome barriers to growth and how it can be used by God to have a significant impact for him in a community.

Yet promoting church health and growth is not easy. One way of not losing what we have discovered comes from this memorable summary:

$$T + L + V = PC^4$$

A Prevailing Church (= PC, that is, a church of *any size* in any culture, but going forward) will be characterized by three realities.

First is great *Teaching* – biblically based, doctrinally sound, Christ-centred, gospel-proclaiming, Spirit-filled and edifying. Remember, we need to work at 'doing our best as workmen approved' (see 2 Timothy 2:15).

Recall the wisdom that encourages you, if you are a preacher/teacher, to get some feedback on your speaking from someone you trust. Listen to other speakers and learn, though without aping them. Read widely, speak to listeners, think carefully, prepare thoroughly and pray a great deal. All communicators of the gospel must learn to improve.

Next is *Volunteers* – God's people released into works of service. I have drawn attention to some of the pressures on churches of different sizes in harnessing people's gifts. Perhaps the most important lesson is to keep painting a gospel-driven vision and not just 'jobs to be done'. Emphasize the *why* and not just the *what*. It's not about neat, efficient schemes, but releasing disciples faithfully to accomplish what the Lord wants.

What connects 'T' and 'V' is *Leadership*. Leaders exemplify, and use the teaching to encourage other believers to get involved in serving Christ with the whole of their life, in their community and in their local church. That's why we started off with leadership lessons. It's only as these are learned and humbly put into practice that the church will both grow, and then move through various size barriers. Good leaders will ensure that growth isn't just about numbers either, but will help develop overall church health and personal discipleship development.

It's massively helpful to recall that when anyone becomes an encourager, there you will find a leader and there you will have followers. Derek Prime, an experienced British preacher, puts it like this: 'An excellent definition of leadership is that it is the ability to encourage and equip other leaders.'[5] Jill Garrett, writing from an extensive experience of helping leaders, comments, 'Effective leaders create a culture . . . where others can flourish.'[6]

A church needs leaders all the way through: leaders of homes (it may be a single mum with two little children), leaders of home groups, leaders of service teams and staff elders and deacons who oversee aspects of church life. Paying attention to this area of church life is vital if the church isn't to be held back by the limited capacity of even the most gifted of God's servants.

These three elements, T, L and V, need to be in harmony if the church is to be effective, whatever its size.

The third issue is to keep gospel-focused, whether we see one congregation growing or plant other churches. We must keep the church growing by gospel-oriented work and not become fixated with issues of internal church life.[7]

Leaders of small churches or new plants can become overwhelmed with the size of the task, or oblivious to it. Consequently, they may spend most of their time feeling like they are struggling, and then settle for what is safe, even if it's small. That's a temptation they will have to resist.

If they do grow to a larger size, leaders and churches can be tempted just to enjoy it while they can, as we saw, rather than press on through other size barriers. Members of awkward-sized churches may resent too much growth, and large churches can easily become overly comfortable places.

In churches of all sizes, members become 'me-oriented' if they lose sight of the gospel. Self-absorption doesn't need much fuel from our individualist culture to take over in church life. Kathy Keller, wife of the American church leader Tim, says this:

> Redeemer [Church] was founded on the principle that 'we are not a church for ourselves, but for people who don't like church.' From the very first days . . . that commitment has been the foundation beneath all of Redeemer's priorities. We have never sought to gather those who already believe, or take people away from other churches, but to address the secular, skeptical New Yorker who would ordinarily not attend church.
>
> Because of this foundational commitment, God has given Redeemer the rare gift of being able to communicate the gospel plausibly and persuasively to people in the most difficult to reach demographic in the country. But this comes with a price. It

means that we must always remind ourselves that we inside
the church are not to put our own likes, dislikes, priorities
and personal agendas ahead of the needs of those outside
the church. *This is difficult to the point of being nearly impossible,*
as the needs and desires of members (for programs and
budget and training and attention from leaders) will always
be more visible and voluble than the needs of people who
aren't even there and mostly are unable to articulate their
spiritual needs.[8]

Believing the gospel, letting the church be empowered and
shaped by it, and ensuring it gets out so that the church *really*
grows all have to be leadership priorities.[9]

Fourthly, we want to see gospel growth. For many, the
biggest challenge is to see actual new converts. Praise God
when this happens. Statistics, though, provide a stark reminder
about the need to re-evangelize the nation.

Total UK church membership for all denominations is
estimated to be 5.2 million by 2015, down from 6 million at
the turn of the millennium. Of those members, about 3.2
million (6.3% of the English population) were at church on
Sunday in 2005, down from 5.4 million (11.7%) in 1979. The
rate of decline may be slowing down for some, but 'the decline
in most churches is accelerating. [This is] . . . very serious.' For
comparison, this is still three times the number of those who
attend League football matches on a weekend, *but* 'It is
estimated that more than twice as many people in Britain go
to IKEA than attend church every Sunday'.[10]

Church watcher and statistician, Peter Brierley, comments,
'The numbers converting to Christianity are far too small to
match the number of deaths.' With 'the proportion of churchgoers 65 and over [being] twice the proportion of this age
group in the population at large', the high level of deaths of

church attendees will continue for a while 'as churchgoing generations of yesteryear die out'.[11]

Alpha is the most recognizable evangelism course 'brand', and over 3 million have attended it in the UK since its inception in the early 1990s. That is quite an achievement![12] Add up all the attendance for other courses as well, and it may have been in the period 1998–2005 that 150,000 extra people started attending church as a result of a course. Wonderful! But Brierley's conclusion to his analysis is candid: 'that twice as many die every year as are converted through courses *constitutes an urgent call to evangelism.*'[13]

Churches of all sizes need to feel this challenge. Larger churches especially, unless they become outward-looking mission centres for their communities, may end up mainly attracting Christians from smaller churches. 'A large part of the growth . . . is from simply moving church . . . especially if those who do move are attracted to the more "successful" (that is, growing) churches.'[14] This must be replaced with genuine gospel growth; it can be!

But don't let the size of the challenge discourage you. You don't need to. Why not?

And . . . *grow!*

Because *God* has given us his gospel, his wisdom and his Spirit. Put those together, and not even the gates of hell can stop the kingdom of his Son advancing (Matthew 16:18). Brave words? True words!

Encouragement in the task is ringing in our ears every step of the way. We do not need to lose heart (Hebrews 12:1–3). We can be confident and leave the results with God. He is the sovereign Lord.

The wisdom of the Bible enables us to do the task more effectively than we have done. Armed with that, we can tackle the challenges and the problems we face with greater understanding and skill. Like Moses, we can listen, learn and then serve more capably than we did before.

Let the Lord be your vision and imagine what your church could look like if it saw gospel growth. Talk about him and his grace and what it feels like when others come to know him. In a book about church size and growth, let the last lesson be: **Don't talk numbers; talk people having life and eternity transformed.**

Remember, the church will grow. It's God's promise. You don't want to miss out!

Discussion questions

1. Reflecting upon all that you have read, pick three positive lessons that have stood out for you. How do these affect your church?
2. Think about the various 'glass-ceiling' problems described. Discuss with other leaders what may be hindering the growth of your church. Come up with specific steps to make achievable, positive changes.
3. As we've seen, growth brings pain, whatever size you are. How can the gospel help you deal with that and also to counter the temptation to be settled at the size you are? What would it take for your church once more to gladly pray that 'the message of the Lord may spread rapidly and be honoured' (2 Thessalonians 3:1)?
4. Complexity and busyness have cropped up many times. Ask yourself: where does the gospel get lost in your life?

Are you too preoccupied with other things? Too
discouraged? Where does the gospel get lost in your
church life? Are too many things happening that are
sapping energies? Is there an unwillingness to change
for the gospel?

5. We have looked a lot at growth in numbers and size.
What might you say to encourage disciples who feel
disheartened by their lack of gospel impact and who
say, 'It all feels so slow and insignificant'?

6. The statistics showed us that most churches are small
and medium-sized. How can you whet their appetite for
growth? What can you say, in the light of what you have
read, to encourage them to have a different mindset,
one which longs to be part of a growing church?

7. List some concrete action points that could help gospel
progress in your church; could it be making the meetings
more welcoming, praying more faithfully for lost people
in your small groups, or encouraging members to see
their friends through new/gospel-affected eyes?

8. Finally, dream out loud where you would love your
church to be in fifteen years' time. Then discuss where
it could be in five years' time, and start thinking what it
would take to get it from here to there.

NOTES

Introduction

1. See Timothy Keller, *Center Church* (Zondervan, 2012) for a brilliant insight into the issues shaping church life and growth. It is a must-read.
2. I had a book by David Beer entitled *50 Ways to Help Your Church Grow* (Kingsway, 1999). I didn't read it for ages because I had an antipathy for what the title seemed to be advocating. It turned out to be very helpful indeed!
3. Peter Brierley, *UK Church Statistics 2005–2015* (ADBC Publishers, 2011), especially section 0.2 Introduction, pp. 1–7. Also, by the same author, *Pulling Out of the Nosedive: A Contemporary Picture of Churchgoing* (Christian Research, 2006).
4. Ian Stackhouse, *The Gospel-driven Church* (Paternoster, 2004), p. 28.
5. See James Collins and Jerry Porras, *Built to Last* (HarperBusiness, 1994), pp. 43–46, where they talk of 'No "Tyranny of the OR" (Embrace the "Genius of the AND")'. See also Acts 6:7.

6. See 1 Timothy 3:4–5: 'He must manage his own family well
   . . . If anyone does not know how to manage his own family,
   how can he take care of God's church?' The 'take care' is a
   word in Greek that is only used in one other place in the New
   Testament; it describes the care that the Good Samaritan
   took over the man he helped. See Luke 10:34. So 'manage'
   and 'care' are not in opposition to one another, properly
   understood. See also James Emery White, *What They Didn't
   Teach You in Seminary* (Baker, 2011).
7. Glynn Harrison, *The Big Ego Trip* (IVP, 2013), p. 192.
8. John Ortberg, 'The "We" We Want to Be', *Leadership Journal*
   (Spring 2010), p. 23, emphasis added.

1. Recognize that size matters

1. Timothy Keller, 'Leadership and Church Size Dynamics',
   Redeemer City to City (2010), p. 1. This is an exceptionally helpful
   summary of some of the leadership issues that churches
   in different size categories face. The article first appeared in
   The Movement Newsletter, and was reprinted in *Cutting Edge*
   (Vineyard USA, Spring 2008). Also see Timothy Keller,
   'Reformed Church Growth', *Presbyterian Network* reprint,
   reporting on the London Presbyterian Conference (June 1988).
2. Figures supplied by the FIEC Office, 39 The Point, Market
   Harborough, LE16 7QU, UK. Details: 18% have 12 members
   or fewer, 45% have 25 members or fewer, 69% have 50
   members or fewer, and 89% of the total numbers of churches
   have 100 members or fewer. Looking at other denominations,
   the average number of members per church varies depending
   on how membership is defined and measured, but 'raw' figures
   are these: Anglican average 80 members per church; Methodist
   41; Free Churches 65, Baptist 60; New Churches 86, Pentecostal
   110, Smaller Denominations 53; Christian Brethren 57; New
   Frontiers International 132; Grace Baptists 37. Source: Peter

Brierley, *UK Church Statistics 2005–2015* (ADBC Publishers, 2011), data for 2010. One suspects that the size variation may be similar for these denominations and groupings of churches, with a small percentage of very large churches, and progressively more at different sizes until there are a lot of small churches in each.

3. Anon, 'Fast Facts about American Religion', *Hartford Institute for Religion Research 2006*, http://hirr.hartsem.edu/research/fastfacts/fast_facts.html. It is worth noting, however, that 'smaller churches draw only 11 per cent of those who attend worship. Meanwhile 50 per cent of churchgoers attended the largest 10% of congregations (350 regular participants and up).'

4. Dave Murrow, 'Why Men Still Hate Going to Church', *Leadership Journal* (Summer 2012), p. 17.

5. Lyle Schaller, 'You Can't Believe Everything You Hear about Church Growth', *Leadership Journal* (Winter 1997), p. 48.

6. See 'The Simple Church Movement' and its associated websites, e.g. www.simplechurch.co.uk or www.simplechurch.com; see also Tony Dale and Felicity Dale, *Simply Church* (Karis Books, 2000).

7. Shawn McMullen, 'Unleashing the Potential of the Smaller Church', in Rebecca Barnes and Lindy Lowry, '7 Startling Facts: An Up Close Look at Church Attendance in America', www.churchleaders.com/pastors/pastor-articles/139575-7-startling-facts-an-up-close-look-at-church-attendance-in-america.html, p. 4.

8. Ed Stetzer, '7 Startling Facts', www.churchleaders.com/pastors/pastor-articles/139575-7-startling-facts-an-up-close-look-at-church-attendance-in-america.html, p. 3.

9. Julian Joyce, ' "Shoebox" homes become the UK norm', www.bbc.co.uk/news/uk-14916580, 14 September 2011. He comments, 'Britain's new-build homes are the smallest in Western Europe and many are too small for family life . . .

RIBA's survey of new-home buyers in 2009 found that more
than half (58%) said there was not enough space for furniture
they owned . . . Nearly 70% said there was not enough
storage for their possessions. Families reported they did not
have enough space to socialise, entertain guests or spend
quiet time in private, with 34% of fully occupied households
[saying] they didn't have enough space to have friends over for
dinner, and 48% saying they did not have enough space to
entertain visitors at all.'

10. Roger Thoman (quoting Frank Viola), says that the average
    lifespan of a 'simple church' is from six months to two years,
    'Frank Viola Answers Questions', http://sojourner.typepad.
    com/house_church_blog/2006/09/frank_viola_ans.html.

11. Richard Holmes, *Firing Line* (Random House, 1985), p. 316,
    emphasis added.

12. See e.g. Bill Donahue and Russ Robinson, *The Seven Deadly
    Sins of Small Group Ministry* (Zondervan, 2002).

13. Richard Holmes, *Firing Line* (Random House, 1985), p. 293,
    emphasis added.

14. Ed Stetzer, '7 Startling Facts', www.churchleaders.com/
    pastors/pastor-articles/139575-7-startling-facts-an-up-close-
    look-at-church-attendance-in-america.html, p. 4.

15. Peter Brierley, *Pulling Out of the Nosedive: A Contemporary
    Picture of Churchgoing* (Christian Research, 2006), p. 197.

16. Jimmy Scroggins and Steve Wright, 'The Math Doesn't Work:
    Why the Future of Church Planting is Bi-Vocational', *9 Marks
    Journal* (January–February 2013), www.9marks.org/journal/
    math-doesnt-work-why-future-church-planting-bi-vocational.

17. Tim Chester and Steve Timmis, *Everyday Church* (IVP, 2011),
    pp. 182–183. They do not define 'church' as such in the book,
    but slip between 'gospel communities', which practise
    baptism and communion, and 'the gathering', which is 'once
    a week' on a Sunday. Maybe the question that would define

which is 'church' is to ask who the elders are, and to whom people submit.

18. Malcolm Gladwell, *The Tipping Point: How Little Things Can Make a Big Difference* (Little Brown, 2000). See also Timothy Keller, 'To Transform a City', *Leadership Journal* (Winter 2011), p. 75.

19. See James Collins and Jerry Porras, *Built to Last* (HarperBusiness, 1994).

20. Lyle Schaller, *The Multiple Staff and the Larger Church* (Abingdon, 1980).

21. Louis G. Parkhurst, *Francis Schaeffer: The Man and His Message* (Kingsway, 1986), pp. 51–52; Edith Schaeffer, *The Tapestry* (Word, 1981), pp. 201–202.

22. Larry Osborne, *Sticky Teams* (Zondervan, 2010), pp. 61–62.

23. David Anderson, '7 Startling Facts', www.churchleaders.com/pastors/pastor-articles/139575-7-startling-facts-an-up-close-look-at-church-attendance-in-america.html, p. 4.

24. See Anon, 'Fast Facts about American Religion'.

25. See Timothy Keller, *Ministries of Mercy* (Presbyterian and Reformed, 1989); *Generous Justice* (Hodder and Stoughton, 2010).

26. Peter Berger, *A Rumour of Angels: Modern Society and the Rediscovery of the Supernatural* (Anchor, 1970).

27. C. S. Lewis, 'On Church Music', *Christian Reflections* (Godfrey Bles, 1967), pp. 129–130.

28. Gordon MacDonald, *Building below the Waterline: Shoring Up the Foundations of Leadership* (Hendrickson, 2011), pp. 173–174.

2. Seek wisdom

1. Francis Schaeffer, *Art and the Bible*, in *The Complete Works of Francis Schaeffer*, vol. 2 (Crossway, 1982), p. 380.

2. See Dennis E. Johnson, 'A Triperspectival Model of Ministry', in John J. Hughes (ed.), *Speaking the Truth in Love: The Theology*

of John M. Frame (Presbyterian and Reformed, 2009), pp. 631–658.

3. Peter Brierley, *Pulling Out of the Nosedive: A Contemporary Picture of Churchgoing* (Christian Research, 2006), pp. 204–206; also see his *Leadership, Vision and Growing Churches: Results from 1,100 Congregations in a Study Sponsored by the Salvation Army* (Christian Research, 2003).

4. See Hugh Whelchel, *How Then Should We Work?* (WestBow, 2012), pp. 29–30, for a helpful summary of teaching on this issue.

5. See the essay by Peter Adam, 'The Preacher and the Sufficient Word', in Chris Green and David Jackman (eds.), *When God's Voice Is Heard* (IVP, 1995), pp. 27–42; Wayne Grudem, *Systematic Theology* (IVP, 1994), pp. 127–138; and John M. Frame, *The Doctrine of the Word of God* (Presbyterian and Reformed, 2010), pp. 220–238.

6. See James Bannerman, *The Church of Christ* (Banner of Truth, 1960, 2 vols; first published 1869), vol. 1, pp. 348–360. See also John Calvin, *Institutes of the Christian Religion* (Westminster Press, 1960, 2 vols; ed. John T. McNeill), vol. 2, Book 4.10.30, p. 1208.

7. Clive Woodward, *Winning* (Hodder and Stoughton, 2004), p. 195.

8. See e.g. Matt Slater, 'Olympics cycling: Marginal gains underpin Team GB dominance', www.bbc.co.uk/sport/0/olympics/19174302, 8 August 2012.

9. Tim Chester, *A Meal with Jesus* (IVP, 2011), especially 'Meals as Enacted Mission', pp. 79–105.

10. Mark Driscoll and Gerry Breshears, *Vintage Church* (Crossway, 2008), p. 148.

11. See Everett C. Rogers with F. Floyd Shoemaker, *Communication of Innovations* (Free Press, 1971), 2nd edition, p. 182. The author's unpublished PhD thesis, in the same field, was entitled 'The Diffusion of Science: The Geographical

Transmission of Natural Philosophy into the English
Provinces 1660–1760' (Cambridge University, 1981).

12. Margot Morrell and Stephanie Capparell, *Shackleton's Way:
Leadership Lessons from the Great Antarctic Explorer* (Nicholas
Brealey Publishing, 2001), pp. 140–143.

13. William Cunningham, *Historical Theology* (Banner of Truth,
1979, 1st edition 1862), vol. 1, pp. 43–78.

14. Grace Community Church, Bedford, 'Constitution',
unpublished leaflet from a section on members' meetings
(Bedford, 1983), pp. 8–9.

3. Act courageously

1. Mark Driscoll and Gerry Breshears, *Vintage Church* (Crossway,
2008), p. 149.

2. James Collins and Jerry Porras, *Built to Last* (HarperBusiness,
1994), pp. 43–46.

3. See Timothy Keller, *Generous Justice* (Hodder and Stoughton,
2010), pp. 78–79; *Ministries of Mercy* (Presbyterian and
Reformed, 1989), pp. 106–107.

4. See Bill Hybels, *Axiom* (Zondervan, 2008), p. 61. Also see his
Courageous Leadership (Zondervan, 2002).

5. Jim Collins, *Good to Great* (Random House, 2001), p. 27.

6. Ibid., p. 193.

7. David Gooding, *True to the Faith* (Hodder and Stoughton,
1990), p. 11. These are the section markers showing how Luke
organizes his narrative:
Acts 6:7: 'So the word of God spread. The number of disciples
in Jerusalem increased rapidly, and a large number of priests
become obedient to the faith.'
Acts 9:31: 'Then the church throughout Judea, Galilee and
Samaria enjoyed a time of peace. It was strengthened; and
encouraged by the Holy Spirit, it grew in numbers, living in
the fear of the Lord.'

Acts 12:24: 'But the word of God continued to increase and spread.'

Acts 16:5: 'So the churches were strengthened in the faith and grew daily in numbers.'

Acts 19:20: 'In this way the word of the Lord spread widely and grew in power.'

Acts 28:30–31: 'For two whole years Paul stayed there . . . Boldly and without hindrance he preached the kingdom of God and taught about the Lord Jesus Christ.'

4. Overcome three practical limits

1. Steve Tibbert with Val Taylor, *Good to Grow* (Authentic Media, 2011), p. 40.
2. Tim Chester, *Unreached* (IVP, 2012).
3. Torsten Hägerstrand, *Innovation Diffusion as a Spatial Process* (University of Chicago Press, 1967; English trans. Allan Pred with Greta Haag). See also Albert-László Barabási, *Linked: How Everything Is Connected to Everything Else and What It Means for Business, Science, and Everyday Life* (Plume / Penguin, 2003).
'Queens Park is one of the most ethnically diverse wards in England . . . Sixty percent of Queens Park is among the 30% most deprived areas in England, and parts are among the 10% and 20% most income deprived.' Bedford Borough Council, Queen's Park Ward Profile, June 2010, www.bedford.gov.uk/ council_and_democracy. Accessed 20 July 2013.
4. Nigel R. Pibworth, *The Gospel Pedlar* (Evangelical Press, 1987), p. 50.
5. See Ray Evans, 'Decisions, Change and Church: A Case Study', unpublished seminar notes (FIEC Leaders' Conference, 4 November 2011), School of Free Church Leadership: Seminar 3. Available from the author.
6. Ray Bowman and Eddy Hall, *When Not to Build* (Baker, 2000).

5. Rise to the challenge

1. John Gray, *Men Are from Mars, Women Are from Venus*
   (HarperCollins, 1992).
   See e.g. R. Freeman, 'Towards Effective Mentoring in General
   Practice', *British Journal of General Practice* 47 (July 1997),
   pp. 457–460; R. Alliot, 'Facilitatory Mentoring in General
   Practice', *British Medical Journal* 313:7060 (28 September 1996);
   Jennifer King, 'Giving Feedback', *British Medical Journal*
   318:7200 (26 June 1999); Donald A. Schön, *The Reflective
   Practitioner: How Professionals Think in Action* (Basic Books,
   1983); Richard Grol and Martin Lawrence, *Quality Improvement
   by Peer Review* (Oxford University Press, 1995).
2. Rick Warren, *The Purpose-driven Church* (Zondervan, 1995),
   is the best-known one. He employs a baseball diamond
   navigation map, describing five 'purpose zones': outreach,
   worship, fellowship, discipleship and service. People attend
   courses, learn skills, develop character, and progress once they
   have mastered a zone. To me, it seems to work best in a large
   setting. It is a sequential journey and takes time to complete.
   People start a journey and move 'around the diagram' until
   they become more competent. A large church can organize
   this and ensure that high-quality training at every level will
   result in steady numbers of disciples finishing the sequence.
   But can smaller churches really wait long enough before
   disciples have completed all they need to before they are fully
   active? The progression from one area to another also struck
   me as a bit arbitrary – aren't they all meant to be happening
   at the same time? See also Will Mancini, *Church Unique: How
   Missional Leaders Cast Vision, Capture Culture, and Create
   Movement* (Leadership Network, 2008). He describes 'Vision
   Pathways' and 'Mission Maps'.
3. Antonia Fraser, *Cromwell: Our Chief of Men* (Weidenfeld and
   Nicolson, 1973), p. 376.

4. See Timothy Keller, *Center Church* (Zondervan, 2012); *The Freedom of Self-forgetfulness* (10 Publishing, 2012). Also see Tim Chester, *You Can Change* (IVP, 2008); Timothy S. Lane and Paul D. Tripp, *How People Change* (New Growth Press, 2006).

5. Jay E. Adams, *More Than Redemption* (Presbyterian and Reformed, 1979), pp. 88–93.

6. See Neil Hudson, *Imagine Church: Releasing Whole-life Disciples* (IVP, 2012). Also see his *Imagine . . . Life on the Frontline: A Six-week Course for Equipping Whole-life Disciples* (LICC, 2012).

7. See e.g. Hugh Whelchel, *How Then Should We Work?* (WestBow, 2012), pp. 8ff.; Tom Wright, *Surprised by Hope* (SPCK, 2007); Allen Wakabayashi, *Kingdom Come: How Jesus Wants to Change the World* (IVP, 2003); Timothy Keller, *Gospel in Life* (Zondervan, 2010); *Center Church*, esp. pp. 29–44; Michael Wittmer, *Heaven Is a Place on Earth: Why Everything You Do Matters to God* (Zondervan, 2004).

6. Grow to maturity

1. Classic Protestantism defined the Ministry of the Word and the Administration of the Sacraments as essential marks of the church, to which some in the Reformed movement added Church Discipline. More recently the 9Marks movement has added its point of view. See e.g. Mark Dever, *Nine Marks of a Healthy Church* (Founders Press, 1997).

2. Glynn Harrison, *The Big Ego Trip* (IVP, 2013), pp. 70–71.

3. See e.g. Thom S. Rainer and Eric Geiger, *Simple Church: Returning to God's Process for Making Disciples* (Broadman and Holman, 2006).

4. Roy Clements, unpublished address given at the Annual Meetings of Grace Baptist Mission, 24 October 1995.

5. Larry Osborne, *Sticky Church* (Zondervan, 2008).

6. Ibid., pp. 149–154, on this important issue.

7. Serve in ministry

1. See Aubrey Malphurs, *Advanced Strategic Planning* (Baker, 2005). The Introduction, pp. 7–19, is exceedingly helpful. The keen-eyed reader will notice the bell-shaped curve again. Much of the rest of a long book, however, felt very removed from most churches I know.
2. Bruce Bugbee, *What You Do Best in the Body of Christ* (Zondervan, 1995). This book is so helpful on this issue.
3. John Maxwell, *The 360° Leader* (Nelson, 2005). See, especially, his section on 'leading up', pp. 84–157.
4. www.leadershipnow.com/leadershipquotes.html. Accessed 21 August 2013.
5. Brian Boley, Richard Underwood, Paul Mallard, Ray Evans and Tim Saunders, *Learn to Lead: Track 3, Understanding Leadership* (FIEC/Good Book Company, 2007), 'Working with Teams', pp. 28–34, and 'Mobilising the Members', pp. 35–38.
6. Walter Wright, *Relational Leadership* (Paternoster, 2000), pp. 160–181.
7. Nick Milton, 'Knoco stories: From the knowledge management frontline', www.nickmilton.com/2009/06/are-you-putting-man-on-moon-or-just.html, 18 June 2009.
8. *MOTD2*, for those not in the know, is a football programme on the BBC.
9. Timothy Keller, 'The Missional Church', occasional paper (Redeemer Presbyterian Church, New York City, June 2001).
10. Rick Warren, *The Purpose-driven Church* (Zondervan, 1995), pp. 369–375.
11. Ray Evans, 'Joining the Church Family: New Members' Course', unpublished outline course notes (Grace Community Church, Bedford, 2009).
12. Ray Bowman and Eddy Hall, *When Not to Build* (Baker, 2000), p. 58.

13. Simon Rowell et al., 'Grace in Action 2012: The Team Ministries' Update', unpublished booklet (Grace Community Church, Bedford, 2012). This booklet is an insight into how team ministry is structured in a growing church. Available from the author.

8. Reach out in mission

1. I am indebted to Timothy Keller for highlighting the structure of Acts 16. He gave a talk at a meeting at St Helen's, Bishopsgate, London in early 2000, but I have not been able to trace the details.

2. Bill Hybels, *Just Walk across the Room* (Zondervan, 2006), pp. 191–192.

3. Dave Bennett, unpublished MA thesis submitted to the University of Sheffield at Cliff College, Calver, Derbyshire, December 2002.
   Dave Bennett, 'A Study of How Adults Become Christians with Special Reference to the Personal Involvement of Individual Christians', unpublished seminar notes (FIEC Pwllheli Conference, 6 April 2005), p. 2.

4. Richard Meryon, unpublished seminar notes, 'Reaching Men' (FIEC Pwllheli Conference, 5 April 2005).

5. Norman Stone, 'Understanding Media', unpublished seminar notes (Grace Baptist Assembly, Child's Hill Baptist Church, London, May 1993).

6. Timothy Keller, 'The Missional Church', occasional paper (Redeemer Presbyterian Church, New York City, June 2001).

7. See Max McLean and Warren Bird, *Unleashing the Word: Rediscovering the Public Reading of Scripture* (Zondervan, 2009) for an invaluable aid into improving this aspect of church life.

8. Timothy Keller, *The Reason for God* (Dutton, 2008), pp. 3–114.

9. Nelson Searcy with Jennifer Dykes Henson, *Fusion: Turning First-time Guests into Fully Engaged Members of Your Church* (Regal, 2007).

10. David Murrow, *Why Men Hate Going to Church* (Nelson, 2005).
11. For further details see www.christianityexplored.org. We have adapted this popular course, which was developed by Rico Tice of All Souls Church, London.
12. For further details, see www.identitycourse.com. This course is produced by Lee McMunn of St John Newland, Hull.
13. Jim Collins, *Good to Great* (Random House, 2001), pp. 164–178.
14. Steve Timmis and Tim Chester, *The Gospel-centred Church* (The Good Book Company, 2002), pp. 59–60.

9. Touch a community
1. Timothy Keller, *Ministries of Mercy* (Presbyterian and Reformed, 1989); John Stott, *Christian Mission in the Modern World* (IVP, 1975); *Issues Facing Christians Today* (Marshalls, 1984); *The Contemporary Christian* (IVP, 1992).
2. Peter Hitchens, 'Britain can no long [sic] afford to pay the extortionate cost of the welfare state', *Mail Online*, 13 January 2013. (Statistics were correct at the time of writing.)
3. See Tim Chester, *Unreached* (IVP, 2012), for some very insightful comments about this issue.
4. Geoff Knott, 'Social Action and Church Growth' (Jubilee+, June 2013), http://jplus.churchinsight.com/Articles/360373/Jubilee_Plus/About_Us/Research/SOCIAL_ACTION_AND.aspx?dm_i=UNP,1KBIO,7TGOHG,5D7CV,1,

10. Transform a life
1. Bill Hybels and Mark Mittelberg, *Becoming a Contagious Christian* (Zondervan/Scripture Press, 1995), pp. 68–172.
2. Rebecca Manley-Pippert, *Out of the Saltshaker and Into the World: Evangelism as a Way of Life* (IVP, 1999), pp. 51–78.
3. Bill Hybels, 'Confessions of an Evangelist' (Willow Creek Association UK 'It Takes a Team' Conference, November

2003); *Just Walk across the Room* (Zondervan, 2006). This is also available as a course.

4. Timothy Keller suggests ten initial steps of 'natural connection'. I have mentioned the first four; the others are: 'Give them a book to read; Share your story; Answer objections and questions; Invite them to a church event; Offer to read the Bible with them; Take them to an explore course.' Timothy Keller, 'Leaders@7: The Gospel-transformed World: A Church with an Evangelistic Dynamic', seminar (Redeemer Presbyterian Church, 27 September 2010), http://sermons. redeemer.com/store/index.cfm?fuseaction=product.display& Product_ID=19291.

5. Dave Bennett, 'A Study of How Adults Become Christians with Special Reference to the Personal Involvement of Individual Christians', unpublished seminar notes (FIEC Pwllheli Conference, 6 April 2005), pp. 2–3, emphasis added.

6. Hybels and Mittelberg, *Becoming a Contagious Christian*, pp. 50ff.

7. Manley-Pippert, *Out of the Saltshaker*, p. 11.

8. Bill Hybels and Mark Mittelberg, *Becoming a Contagious Christian Training Course: Participant's Guide* (Zondervan, 1995), pp. 26–32. Also see Mark Mittelberg, *Building a Contagious Church* (Zondervan, 2000), pp. 247–338.

9. Hybels and Mittelberg, *Becoming a Contagious Christian Training Course*, pp. 64–67. The 'bridge diagram' starts with God creating us, but because of our rebellion, a chasm has opened up between us. People often reach out for 'something missing' in life, but our attempts to connect to God fail and we all are under his judgment, which death confirms. The good news is that God has built a bridge back! Christ, the God-man, spans the chasm, and by his death on the cross takes the judgment for us. We are called to trust wholly in Christ and his work as we return 'across the bridge' to God, and begin a new relationship with him.

10. See Timothy Keller, *Center Church* (Zondervan, 2012), pp. 32–44, for more examples of engaging with people using the Bible's narrative structure and themes. See also Tim Chester, *Unreached* (IVP, 2012), pp. 99–117, for further helpful ways of talking to people naturally, but with some structure in what you say.

11. Faith Cook, *Fearless Pilgrim: The Life and Times of John Bunyan* (Evangelical Press, 2008), pp. 83–85, quoting from John Bunyan's autobiographical *Grace Abounding* (1666), para. 37.

12. London Institute for Contemporary Christianity, *Imagine . . . Life on the Frontline* (LICC, 2012); Hybels, *Just Walk across the Room*.

11. Get ready to grow

1. See John Burke, *Mud and the Masterpiece: Seeing Yourself and Others through the Eyes of Jesus* (Baker, 2013).

2. John Burke, *No Perfect People Allowed: Creating a Come-As-You-Are Culture in the Church* (Zondervan, 2005).

3. Bill Hybels, *Courageous Leadership* (Zondervan, 2002), p. 12.

4. Bill Hybels, 'The Leader's Edge' (Willow Creek Association UK 'Building Life-changing Churches' Conference, April 2002).

5. Derek Prime, *A Christian's Guide to Leadership – for the Whole Church* (Evangelical Press, 2005), p. 85.

6. Jill Garrett quoted in Peter Brierley, *Pulling Out of the Nosedive: A Contemporary Picture of Churchgoing* (Christian Research, 2006), p. 204.

7. See Colin Marshall and Tony Payne, *The Trellis and the Vine* (Matthias Media, 2009). There is a lot of wisdom in what they say, but I do feel that they play down 'Kingly' leadership.

8. Kathy Keller, 'How to Be Happy at Redeemer', *Redeemer Report* (April 2013), emphasis added, www.redeemer.com/ news_and_events/newsletter/?aid=461.

9. Brierley, *Pulling Out of the Nosedive*, p. 201.

10. Peter Brierley, *UK Church Statistics 2005–2015* (ADBC Publishers, 2011), p. 2; *Pulling Out of the Nosedive*, pp. 13–14.

11. Peter Brierley, 'Census Sense', *FutureFirst*, no. 25 (February 2013), pp. 1–2.

12. Brierley, *Pulling Out of the Nosedive*, p. 231.

13. Ibid., p. 209, emphasis added.

14. Ibid., p. 203.

related titles from IVP

Fruitful Leaders
How to make, grow, love and keep them
Marcus Honeysett

ISBN: 978-1-84474-544-9
216 pages, paperback

God loves local churches. He wants to see them built up and flourishing. He provides spiritual gifts of leadership to help them grow. Churches are God's teams for fulfilling his great purposes in the world, ensuring that his greatness and glory, and the good news of his grace, are received and rejoiced in everywhere.

God wants to raise up leaders in your local church in all kinds of spheres and activities. But this book is for everyone, not just for leaders or potential leaders. In fact, the whole congregation should be asking how they can release those gifted by God to lead, to the fullest extent of their ability. This book is ideal for anyone asking whether God could use them as a leader in a home group, youth group, or indeed any other church activity. It will also offer fresh vision to existing leaders, and inspire those who are cultivating a fresh crop of new leaders.

'The ideas here are radical as well as utterly biblical and practical ... this book provides a refreshing and realistic agenda for healthy and productive change in churches large and small.'
Jonathan Lamb

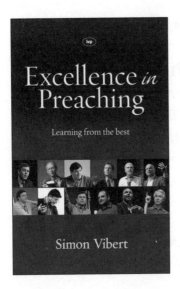

related titles from IVP

Excellence in Preaching
Learning from the best
Simon Vibert

ISBN: 978-1-84474-519-7
176 pages, paperback

What makes some preaching gripping – unforgettable even?
What can we learn from the best preachers?
How can we appreciate great preaching, often at the click of a mouse, without devaluing the role of the local church minister?

'Without creating a guru mentality, I focus on one positive aspect from each preacher and offer ideas on how other preachers might emulate them,' says author Simon Vibert. He also looks at the Bible's own take on good preaching, and focuses on the exemplary models of Jesus and Paul.

This is not a how-to manual, nor a biblical theology of preaching, nor even a critique of the subjects. Rather, it is a focus on modern-day practitioners, from whom all preachers can form a composite picture of excellence, and from whom all preachers would do well to learn.

'An inspiring, accessible and engaging book for preachers, at whatever stage in their preaching ministry ... A must-read for anyone who takes preaching seriously.' Revd Clare Hendry

Available from your local Christian bookshop or **www.thinkivp.com**

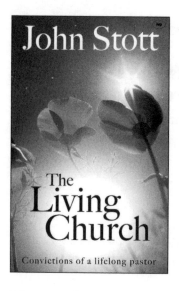

related titles from IVP

The Living Church
*Convictions of
a lifelong pastor*
John Stott

ISBN: 978-1-84474-183-0
192 page paperback

What exactly is a living church?

Author John Stott explains, *'We need more radically
conservative churches: "conservative" in the sense that they
conserve what Scripture plainly requires, but radical in relation
to that combination of tradition and convention that we call
"culture". Scripture is unchangeable, but culture is not.'*

The Living Church brings together a number of characteristics
of what the author calls 'authentic' or 'living' church.
The marks, being clearly biblical, are timeless and need
to be preserved.

We are encouraged to become learning, caring, worshipping
and evangelizing churches.

John Stott unpacks the Bible's wisdom rigorously with a
teacher's skill and applies it faithfully with a pastor's heart.
Becoming a living church is not an impossible goal.

Available from your local Christian bookshop or **www.thinkivp.com**